500

crochet blocks

500

crochet blocks

the only compendium of crochet blocks you'll ever need

Hannah Elgie & Kath Webber

Search Press

A Quintet Book

First published in the UK in 2013 by
Search Press Ltd
Wellwood
North Farm Road
Tunbridge Wells
Kent TN2 3DR
United Kingdom

www.searchpress.com

Reprinted 2013, 2014, 2015

ISBN: 978 1 84448 932 9
QTT.CBLK

This book was conceived, designed, and produced by
Quintet Publishing Limited
6 Blundell Street
London N7 9BH
United Kingdom

Photographer: Lydia Evans
Project Editor: Margaret Swinson
Pattern Consultant: Carol Meldrum
Designer: Tania Field
Technical Designer: Gareth Butterworth
Art Director: Michael Charles
Editorial Director: Donna Gregory
Publisher: Mark Searle

The authors would like to thank their husbands, Joe and Darryl, their
children, Albert and Lily-Beatrice, all the creative women who've
helped with this book, Carol Meldrum, Amy, Kerry, Nastassia, Jo, Sue,
Marion, Mell, Helen and Caroline, and the hard-working team at
Quintet.

10 9 8 7 6 5

Printed in China by 1010 Printing International Ltd.

contents

introduction

This is the ultimate compendium for beginner, intermediate and advanced crocheters. Use this guide as an introduction to the basics of the craft, and work through the blocks to learn all the stitches you'll ever need to know, with a few professional hints and tips along the way.

The first thing to understand about crochet is that it can become an addiction – but let's face it, there are much worse addictions! Like its sister craft, knitting, crochet is satisfying, beautiful and useful. With just a few simple and inexpensive tools (a hook, some yarn, a creative mind and a little patience), you can create something wonderful from very little. Crochet lends itself to making dresses and baby booties as well as things for the home. From doilies and afghans to coasters and pot holders, crochet is a really versatile skill to have.

Crochet is a relatively new type of needlecraft, having only been popularized in the nineteenth century. 'Crochet' comes from the French word for 'hook', and with this single tool you can make any number of things. Combining a variety of stitches can result in thousands of possibilities, and this book will teach you the basic techniques behind them. It also outlines 500 different crochet blocks, taking you from beginner- right up to advanced-level blocks, and gives you the skills to create some stunning crocheted items. Have fun!

how to use this book

Each pattern features 6 crochet blocks and suggestions for how to use them. The main pattern teaches the basic techniques of the block, and then there are 5 variations offering alternatives to the main pattern and providing complementary blocks to mix and match. The main skills you'll learn are as follows:

crocheting back and forth

Crocheting blocks doesn't just mean granny square motifs. Create perfect squares by starting with a foundation chain and then working back and forth along this chain, as well as by increasing and decreasing to make shapes and patterns.

crocheting in the round

Use this essential technique and go on to include any colour changes, working the foundation ring and creating perfect squares – in the round!

working with colour

This section will show off your skills in glorious Technicolor! Learn about colour changing methods and which patterns work best in multiple colours, such as stripes and diagonal patterns.

shaped motifs

Using stars, circles, hearts and hexagons that can be tessellated (repeated use of a single shape, without gaps or overlapping) and joined, you can make scarves, blankets and decorative items with these amazing shapes. All the basic skills in the first chapter can be applied to create advanced patterns for shaped blocks in the final chapter. There is advice on making the projects, but see pages 24–25 for a more comprehensive guide to joining and finishing your work.

techniques and equipment

essential kit

Once you have chosen to embark on a crochet odyssey, you'll need a few things to get you on your way. A local knitting or yarn store will almost certainly be able to get you started with some equipment for crocheting, but don't underestimate the shopping potential of the internet. There are hundreds, possibly thousands, of online craft stores that carry all the items you'll ever need. Build a good relationship with your local yarn store – it's great to support your community. They might even be able to suggest crochet social groups and outings, or even offer classes or workshops to improve your skills. You'll need the following items to get started:

crochet hooks: These come in various sizes, from 1mm for tiny and intricate lace work, up to large 15mm and even 25 or 30mm hooks for big works. We recommend starting with a 4mm hook (size G), for standard knitting yarn (called double knitting or 8 ply). If you want to start with a larger hook and thicker yarn, this might help you to see the stitches more clearly. You'll need a 5mm (size H) or 6mm (size J) hook for aran (worsted) weight yarn or an 8mm (size L) hook for bulky (chunky) yarn.

yarn: (see page 10).

notions: These include **scissors** for cutting yarn, a large, blunt **darning needle** for sewing in ends, **stitch markers** or **clips**.

Any other haberdashery items or embellishments in your sewing box can be used to adorn your work. These can include **buttons, beads** and **sequins**.

a note about yarn

Once you have decided to learn to crochet, the fun part is choosing your yarn. Don't be restricted by what the pattern says; if you have seen some sumptuous yarn on sale, then go for it! All the blocks in this book have suggested yarn to use and that is the yarn used for the example block. However, you need not be restricted to that yarn at all – you can substitute almost any yarn as long as you use the right size hook. If you're making a granny square and you want it thick and chunky, use a chunky weight yarn or wool. Or if you want tiny, delicate ones then use a 4 ply or lace weight yarn instead. You don't need to use crochet cotton for your crochet, you can use any material. Even torn-up old sheets can be given a new lease of life with giant crochet hooks! To help you, here is a basic chart so you have the right tools for the job. Check the band on the yarn first for needle and hook size suggestions, but if you're not sure, then check below.

more stitches

yarn weight	hook size (metric)	(letter)
4 ply (fingering or sock yarn)	2.25mm	B
8 ply/double knitting (also known as DK)	3.5mm/4mm	E/G
aran (worsted)	5mm/5.5mm/6mm	H/I/J
bulky (also known as chunky)	6mm/8mm	J/L
super bulky (also known as super chunky)	10mm/12mm	N/P
hoopla yarn	8mm/9mm/10mm/11mm/12mm	L/M/N/O/P

how to crochet

Take some time over these instructions, and remember that practice makes perfect. These can easily work whether you are left- or right-handed – use the hook in the hand that you write with. You can hold it like a pencil, or with the hook underneath your hand. Hold the hook however feels comfortable – there is no 'right' or 'wrong' way.

slip knot

To begin almost all crochet, you'll need to make a slip knot. You will need to have a longish bit of yarn ready. Make a loop with the yarn and pull the tail end (the end not attached to the ball of yarn) through and tighten. Pop that slip knot onto the crochet hook and tug sharply to pull it tight.

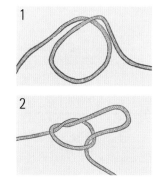

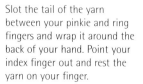

holding the yarn

Once the slip knot is on the hook, hold your left hand out, palm up, or vice versa if you are left-handed. There are 2 ways of holding the yarn, shown as A and B at right.

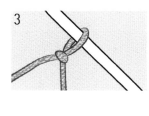

Slot the tail of the yarn between your pinkie and ring fingers and wrap it around the back of your hand. Point your index finger out and rest the yarn on your finger.

Another method of holding the working yarn is to wrap it twice around your index finger.

making a chain

The foundation chain is the beginning of almost all the blocks in this book. Once done, it resembles a braid or a series of 'V' shapes.

Bring the hook under the yarn that rests on your index finger. Clasp the yarn around the hook and pull it through the loop on the hook. Repeat this until you have the desired amount of stitches. Count each chain stitch as you work them but do not count the loop on your hook.

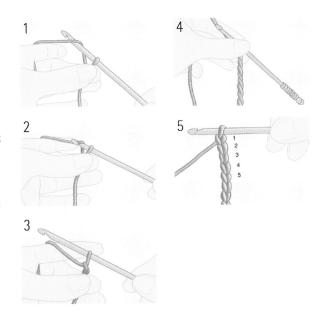

how to slip stitch

This stitch is used for joining, or working along to the next point in the pattern while being invisible. As you did for the foundation chain, insert the hook through the stitch and wrap the yarn over hook (YOH) by bringing your hook under the yarn resting on your finger and drawing it through the loop. You'll now have 2 loops on your hook. Draw the first one through the second one, leaving you with 1 loop on the hook.

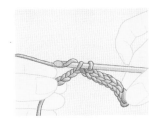

double crochet

This small stitch is tight and neat, perfect for working with shaped motifs. One side of your foundation chain will have a series of little 'V's.

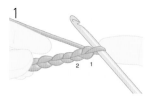

After you have made the foundation chain, count the stitches back from the hook. Insert the hook into the second "V" along the hook.

Wrap the yarn around the hook and draw it back through this stitch. You will now have 2 loops on the hook.

Wrap the YOH again and draw it through both loops on the hook. You have a made a single crochet! Continue into every stitch until you get to the end of the foundation row.

To work the next row, chain 1 and turn your work. Insert your hook into the first stitch under the top 2 loops and complete steps 2 and 3. Continue working single crochet stitches across the row. You do not work a stitch into the turning chain of the previous row.

Yarn over and draw it through both loops on your hook to complete the stitch. Insert your hook into the next chain and complete steps 4 and 5. Repeat into each chain across.

1 loop stitch made.

treble crochet

This is probably the most common crochet stitch, and produces a long, sturdy stitch perfect for making large blocks.

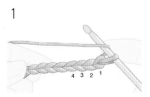

1

Yarn over and insert your hook into the fourth chain from your hook.

2

Yarn over and pull up a loop. You will have 3 loops on your hook.

3

Yarn over and draw through 2 loops. You will have 2 loops on your hook.

4

Yarn over and draw through 2 loops to complete the stitch. Yarn over, insert your hook into the next chain, and complete steps 2 to 4. Repeat into each chain across.

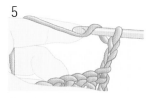

5

To work the next row, chain 3 and turn your work. Insert your hook into the second stitch (skipping the first stitch because the chain 3 counts as a stitch.) Work under the top 2 loops and complete steps 2 to 4.

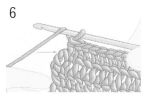

6

Continue working stitches into each stitch across the row. Your last stitch will be made into the top chain of the previous row's turning chain.

double treble crochet

This is a long, loose stitch which crochets up quickly. Wrap the yarn around the hook TWICE, and then insert the hook into the stitch required. With YOH, pull loop back through stitch. There are now 4 loops on the hook. YOH, pull through first 2 loops, YOH, pull through next 2 loops, YOH, and pull through final 2 loops on hook.

triple treble crochet

This is very long and loose – it's not used frequently, but it is handy for creating height and lacy stitches. Wrap the yarn around the hook 3 times, and then insert the hook into the required stitch. With YOH, pull loop back through stitch. You now have 5 loops on the hook. YOH, pull through first 2 loops, YOH, pull through next 2 loops, YOH, pull through next 2 loops, YOH, pull through last 2 loops.

turning chain

You will need to work some extra chains at the end of each row or round for turning – how many chains will depend on what stitch you are doing. The turning chain ensures there are enough stitches in the row overall, so add the following number of extra chains on your foundation to make sure you have enough stitches in the row:

For double crochet, 1 chain

For treble crochet, 3 chains

For double treble crochet, 4 chains

For triple treble, 5 chains

You will also work a turning chain at the beginning of each row. **This will count as the first stitch of your round or row.** Some crocheters find it simple to work the turning chain BEFORE turning their work, but only do this when working back and forth along the foundation chain.

half treble crochet

YOH, insert hook into stitch. YOH, draw loop through stitch so there are 3 loops on the hook. YOH, draw yarn up through all 3 stitches on hook.

half double treble crochet

YOH twice, insert hook into stitch. YOH, draw loop through stitch so there are 4 loops on the hook. YOH, draw yarn up though all 4 loops on hook.

increase

To increase the amount of stitches in a row, simply work 2 or more stitches into 1 stitch on the previous row.

decreasing

To decrease stitches, sometimes you'll be instructed to simply skip a stitch and work over the skipped stitch into the next one. However, there is a simple and often-used method of crocheting 2 stitches together on 1 row to create just 1 stitch on the row above. This is normally a treble crochet of 2 stitches together. YOH, insert hook into stitch, YOH, draw yarn up through stitch. YOH, draw yarn through 2 loops on hook. YOH, insert hook into the NEXT stitch, YOH, drawn yarn back up through the stitch. YOH, draw yarn through 2 loops on hook, YOH, draw yarn through all the remaining loops on the hook. What you're doing is working the first part of the stitch into 1 stitch, then working the first part of the stitch into the next stitch, then bringing them together. This will make a little upside-down 'V' shape on your row. You can work 2 double treble crochet stitches together in the same way.

front post crochet

Insert the hook around the stitch on the row below from right to left, pushing the stitch to the front of the hook. Work stitch as usual.

back post crochet

Insert the hook around the stitch, from the back – right to left – pushing the stitch BEHIND the hook. Work the stitch as usual.

working in the round

As well as working a chain and joining it with a slip stitch, there are two other ways of making a circle:

Magic circles These are ideal for closing tight centres. In this case, you simply wrap the tail of the yarn around your index finger, then tuck the end underneath as shown below.

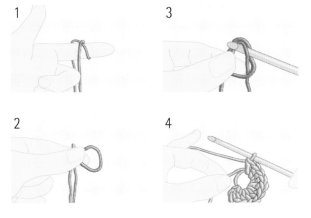

Hold the 'magic circle' tightly between your thumb and forefinger on your yarn hand while you work the first few stitches for your foundation round. Join the round with a slip stitch and pull the yarn end tightly to close the circle.

Chain 2 Work the stitches into the second chain from the hook then join with a slip stitch. Pull the yarn end tightly to close the circle.

textural stitches

cluster stitch

You can work any number of stitches into the same original stitch (or 'V') and create a cluster stitch. Typically, 3-treble crochet stitches will be gathered together to form a cluster stitch. However in this book, there are examples of 4-treble crochet cluster stitches and also 3-double treble crochet cluster stitches. To make a 3-treble crochet cluster stitch:

YOH, insert hook into stitch, YOH, draw yarn back up through stitch to get 3 loops on hook. YOH, pull yarn through the first 2 loops on the hook. Leave 1 loop remaining on hook. YOH, insert hook back into the SAME stitch as before, YOH, and draw yarn back through the stitch. There are now 4 loops on the hook. YOH, draw yarn through first 2 loops. Leaving 2 loops on the hook, YOH and insert hook back into the same original stitch again. YOH, draw yarn through stitch, leaving 5 loops on the hook. YOH, draw yarn through first 2 loops. YOH once more, and draw this loop through the remaining loops on your hook. Essentially, you're working the first part of a treble crochet (open treble crochet), and then starting over into the same stitch. For examples, see pages 79, 142, 169.

bobble stitch

Like a cluster stitch, work 4-open treble crochet stitches into the same stitch: YOH, insert hook into stitch, YOH, draw loop back through stitch, YOH, draw yarn through 2 loops on hook, leaving 5 loops on the hook. YOH, draw through all 5 loops on hook. For examples, see pages 55, 190.

puff stitch

Again, you can work in any number of stitches to form a puff stitch, which is, as the name suggests, a very textural stitch. This instruction is for a typical puff stitch made of 4 treble crochets. Wrap the YOH, insert the hook into the required stitch, YOH, draw yarn back up through the stitch so there are 3 loops on the hook. Repeat this process 4 times, so there are 7 loops on the hook. YOH, draw loop though all the remaining loops on the hook. Chain 1 stitch to 'lock' or close the puff stitch. For an example, see page 116.

popcorn stitch

A popcorn stitch is a group of treble crochet stitches that are folded together and closed at the top. The pattern will tell you to work a number of treble crochet stitches into the required stitch. Remove the hook from the loop, leaving the loop relatively loose. Insert the hook into the top of the first treble crochet of the group, and pick up the loop from the final treble crochet of the group. Pull this loop through the loop on the hook to close the popcorn. For an example, see page 197.

spike stitch

Spike stitches can be made in any stitch, but are usually made in double crochet. Insert the hook into the same stitch one or more rows below, YOH, draw the loop back through the stitch, YOH, draw through 2 loops on hook. For examples, see pages 64, 169.

bullion stitch

Wrap the yarn around the hook 7 times (or as many times you like), then insert hook into the stitch. YOH, draw the loop back through the stitch, then gently draw yarn through ALL loops on the hook. Work 1 double crochet to secure. For examples, see pages 72, 141.

extended double crochet

Insert hook into stitch, YOH, pull through 1 loop, and you'll have 2 loops on the hook. YOH, pull through 2 loops. For an example, see page 51.

reading a pattern

The patterns in this book are written in abbreviations, all of which can be found in the chart below. Follow the instructions in the pattern, using this guide to work out the stitches used in the pattern.

full stitch name	abbreviation
double crochet	dc
treble crochet	tr
double treble crochet	dtr
triple treble crochet	trtr
quadruple treble crochet	quadtr
half treble crochet	htr
half double treble crochet	hdtr
chains(s)	ch(s)
slip stitch	ss
skip (1 stitch)	sk
right side	rs
wrong side	ws
spike stitch	sp st
cluster stitch	cl
puff stitch	ps
bobble stitch (make bobble)	mb

full stitch name	abbreviation
bullion stitch	bs
treble crochet 2 stitches together	tr2tog
double treble crochet 2 stitches together	dtr2tog
front post treble crochet/ front post double treble crochet	fptr/fpdtr
back post treble crochet/ back post double treble crochet	bptr/bpdtr
double crochet 2 stitches together	dc2tog
increase	inc
decrease	dec
yarn over hook	yoh
loops	lp(s)

reading a chart

Using a crochet chart is really simple. Use this key to decipher the charts in this book. Please note that the charts in this book apply only to the main blocks and not the variations.

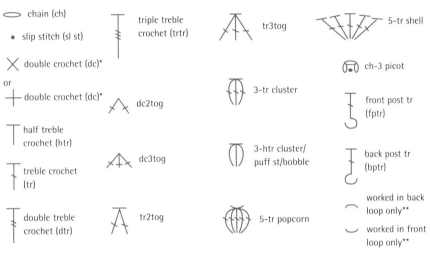

* both symbols are commonly used for double crochet
** symbols appear at base of stitch being worked

UK term	pattern term	US term	pattern term
double crochet	dc	single crochet	sc
half treble crochet	htrc	half double crochet	hdc
treble crochet	trc	double crochet	dc
double treble	dtrc	treble crochet	tr
triple treble	ttrc	double treble	dtrc

finishing your work

Finishing your work properly is often essential to the longevity and visual appeal of your crochet.

To fasten off your work, simply pull the loop that is on the hook nice and loose, and pass the working yarn through the loop, pulling tightly to make a neat knot. Fastening off in this way ensures an invisible join. Cut off the working yarn, leaving a tail of around 7.5 cm (3 in) long.

To make the yarn ends disappear, you'll need to weave them into the work. Thread your darning needle, and pass the needle through the back of the stitches on the wrong side of the work, so you cannot see the weave from the front. Pass through as many stitches as you like to ensure an invisible end. Cut yarn if necessary.

blocking and shaping

Blocking your work is the act of shaping it, and it's worth doing this to make the most of your work. The majority of blocks in this book can, and should, be blocked. It doesn't take long and really ensures that the shape and construction of the work is shown how it should be. Some shapes and fibres can simply be pulled into shape, but other shapes will benefit from blocking – particularly shaped blocks or those with curved edges (usually when a block is crocheted in double crochet).

For light blocking, lay the work out to its true shape and pin it. You can pin it to a folded towel or an ironing board. Place a damp cloth over the work and press lightly on a cool iron. Check the yarn label for care advice – some acrylic yarns should not be ironed.

For heavy blocking, usually with natural fibres, lay the work out and pin it. Saturate the work with water or spray starch for a stiff finish, using a spray bottle or something similar. Leave the work somewhere warm until it is totally dry. Remove the pins.

joining blocks

Joining blocks together is a great way of making projects, elevating crochet to much more than just the sum of its parts. The easiest way of joining blocks together is to use matching yarn and a darning needle.

First, lay out the blocks and decide which order they will go in. If you can, leave them on the floor or table in this order so that you can keep track. Or take a photograph to refer back to if you're joining lots of blocks together. Work in rows, joining the top row together block by block. Once all the horizontal rows are joined together, you can join the vertical rows.

sewing blocks together

woven stitch Match the stitches on the blocks up, and work the needle through the stitches, passing the needle back and forth through the stitches all the way down.

back stitch Match the stitches up on both blocks, and work a back stitch seam for a firm join.

simple over stitch Match the stitches up on the sides of the blocks, then work the needle round over each stitch to join. For an almost invisible join, work through the back loop of the stitch.

crocheting blocks together

slip stitch Match up the seams. Use a crochet hook, insert the hook into the stitches on both blocks and pull the yarn back through. Slip this loop through the loop on the hook. Repeat into each stitch all the way along.

double crochet Whether using matching yarn or contrasting yarn, this will make a strong seam with a slight texture. Match up the stitches, insert the hook into the first stitch, YOH, and pull back through stitches. YOH, draw through both loops on hook. Repeat all the way along.

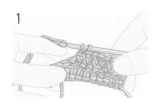

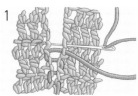

edgings

Blankets, scarves, and afghans all look beautiful with edgings. Here are some simple suggestions:

double crochet Using matching or contrasting yarn, work several rows/rounds of double crochet around the edge for a solid, simple edging.

picot edge Makes a simple, pretty edge. Chain 3, insert hook into the 3rd chain from the hook, YOH, draw through the stitch and the loop on the hook. Double crochet into the next stitch. Repeat picot, double crocheting along.

looped edge Chain 5, skip 5 stitches, double crochet into the next stitch.

shell edge Skip 2 stitches, work 5-treble crochet into the next stitch, skip 2 stitches, work 1 double crochet into the next stitch.

granny edge Chain 3, work 2-treble crochet stitches into the same stitch. Skip 2 stitches, work 3-treble crochet into the next, repeat, work 3-treble crochet, chain 3, then 3-treble crochet into the corners.

tassels Fringing is very simple. Cut 4 pieces of yarn of equal lengths. Fold all 4 pieces in half, insert the hook into the stitch, and grab the fold with the hook. Pull through one half of the folded yarn. Tie in a knot to close.

essential hints and tips

- When working the stitches, you typically work each stitch into the top of the stitches on the row below. If you look at the crochet from above, you'll see a series of 'V's that look like the chain. Insert the hook just under the 'V', which will be working into the top 2 loops of the stitch.

- When working with back and forth patterns, you'll need to turn the work at the end of a row. Flip your crochet from left to right 180 degrees, so that the hook is now on the right-hand side of the row.

- Working into just the front loop or just the back loop of the stitch will give you a ribbed, ridged effect, and the crocheted item will not lie flat.

- There is often a right side and wrong side in crochet. They look different, but can be equally attractive. When working with back and forth patterns, alternate rows will be worked with the right side facing. In most patterns worked in the round, you'll be crocheting with the right side facing.

- When working in rounds, you'll usually (though not always) begin with a foundation chain. Join the chain into a loop by inserting the hook into the very first chain made, YOH, then pull this loop through the yarn on the hook. This is slip stitching the chain together to form a loop. You will finish each round in the same way, inserting the hook into the first stitch worked, and drawing the yarn through the loop on the hook to slip stitch the edges together.

- Changing colour is usually done at the end of the row, but can also be done mid-row. The technique is the same. Let the working yarn fall behind the work. Wrap the new colour around your hand, and make a loop through the loop on the hook. Pull the tail of the old colour tight. You now have the new colour as your working yarn. Tie the tails into a small tight knot behind the work to secure.

- To save time if weaving in ends when you're working in colour, work in the ends as you go. When you change colour, cut your tail ends the same length, then hold them along the top of the previous row. When you work the next row, the stitches will capture the ends and conceal them.

back and forth

In this chapter you will be able to use the basic
stitches of crochet in many different patterns.
Whether you are new to crochet or are brushing
up on existing skills, you can create a variety of
blocks in an endless array of colours. You may
prefer to use the written instructions or
the crochet diagrams as you start your journey
with crochet.

solid weave

Main pattern: Using yarn A, ch21.

Row 1: 1dc into 2nd ch from hook, 1dc into each ch to end, turn (20sts).

Row 2: ch1, 1dc into first st, 1dc into each st to end.

Repeat Row 2 a further 22 times.

materials

- 4mm hook: main, Var 1-4
- Debbie Bliss Cotton DK
  sh61 Aqua (A), sh20 Apple
  Green (B), sh19 Pigeon (C),
  sh52 Earth (D)
- 9mm hook: Var 5
- hoopla yarn

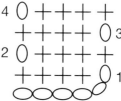

see other variations page 92

variation 1
Treble crochet Using yarn B, ch23. Row 1: 1tr into 4th ch from hook, 1tr into each ch to end, turn (20sts). Row 2: ch3, 1tr into first st, 1tr into each st to end, turn. Repeat Row 2 11 more times.

shelley

Main pattern: Multiple of 6+6 (add 3 for turning ch). Using yarn A, ch28.

Row 1: 2tr in 4th ch from hook, * sk2ch, 1dc into the next ch, sk2ch, 5tr into next ch, 1dc into next ch, rep from * ending with 3tr into last ch, turn.

Row 2: 5tr into first dc of previous row, * sk2, 1dc in next st (centre st of 5tr), sk2, 5tr into next st, rep from * ending last rep with dc into top of tch, turn.

Row 3: ch3, 2tr into 1st st, * sk2, 1dc into next st (centre of 5tr), sk2, 5tr into next st, rep from * ending last rep with 3tr into top of tch, turn.

Rows 2-3 form the pattern; repeat to required length.

materials

- 4mm hook
- Sublime Baby Cashmere Merino Silk DK in Button (A), Teddy (B), Raffia (C)
- wooden beads

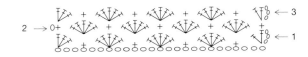

see other variations page 93

variation 1

Wavy Work as given for main pattern, using yarn A for Row 1 and yarn B for Row 2, keeping stripe sequence as set throughout.

ribbed and ridged

Main pattern: Using yarn A, ch23.

Row 1: 1tr into 4th ch from hook, 1tr into each ch to end, turn.

Row 2: ch3, 1tr into back loop of first st, 1tr into back loop of each st to end, 1tr into top of tch, turn.

Row 2 forms pattern; repeat to required length.

Project notes: Hairband.
Ch13 and work to desired length in treble crochet. Make a bow as follows: ch5, work 3tr into 1st ch, turn, ch4, 3tr, ch4 into same ch. Fasten off, leaving a long chain. Wrap chain around the bow's centre several times. Attach to headband.

materials

- ▩ 4mm hook
- ▩ King Cole Bamboo Cotton in Yellow (A), Oyster (B), Blush (C), Aqua (D), Peacock (E)

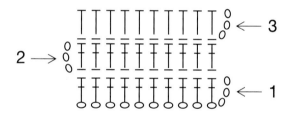

---

variation 1

see other variations page 94

Wobbly Using yarn B, ch23. Work as given for main pattern, working Row 1 into front loop of stitch and Row 2 into back loop, then Row 3 into front loop. Rows 2–3 form pattern; repeat to required length.

fan stitch

Main pattern: Using yarn A, ch21.

Row1: 5dtr into the 4th ch from the hook, * sk2ch, 1tr into next ch, sk2ch, 5dtr in next ch, rep from * ending 1tr in last ch, turn.

Row 2: ch3, 2dtr in 1st tr, * sk2, 1tr in next dtr (centre dtr of 5), sk2, 5dtr in next tr, rep from * ending 3dtr in ch1, turn.

Row 3: ch1, sk3, * 5dtr in next tr, sk2, 1tr in next dtr (centre dtr of 5), sk2 , rep from * ending 1tr in top of tch, turn.

Rows 2–3 form pattern, repeat to required length.

materials

- 4mm hook: main, Var 1-4
- King Cole Smooth Double Knit in Raspberry (A), Blue (B), Grey (C), Green (D)
- 10mm hook: Var 5
- hoopla yarn

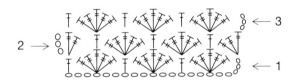

see other variations page 95

variation 1

Half-and-half colour Work as given for main pattern, working Rows 1–5 in yarn A and Rows 6–10 in yarn B.

dorothy

Main pattern: work ib multiples of 16+1 for turning ch. Using yarn A, ch17.

Row 1: ch1, 1dc into 2nd ch from hook, then 1dc into each st to end, turn (17sts).

Row 2: ch3, sk2, 1tr into next st, then work 1tr into last skipped st, enclosing the 1st tr worked, * sk1, 1tr into next, 1tr into skipped st. Repeat from * to end. Work 1tr into top of turning chain, turn.

Row 2 forms pattern; repeat to required length.

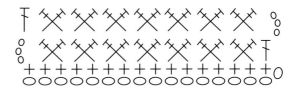

see other variations page 96

variation 1

Closed crossed treble crochet Using yarn C, work Rows 1–2 as given for main pattern. Row 3: ch1, sk1, 1dc into each st to end, turn. Row 4: work as Row 2. Rows 2–4 form pattern; repeat to required length.

ripples and waves

Main pattern: work in multiples of 14, plus 3 for a turning chain. Using yarn A, ch28+3.

Row 1: 1tr into 4th ch from hook, 1tr into next 4ch, * (tr2tog) twice (decrease worked), 1tr into next 4ch, (2tr into next ch) twice (increase worked), 1tr into next 4ch, rep from * ending last rep after 1st set of 2tr into next ch, turn.

Row 2: ch3 (counts as 1tr), 1tr into base of ch3, 1tr into next 4sts, * (tr2tog) twice (decrease worked), 1tr into next 4sts, (2tr into next st) twice (increase worked), 1tr into next 4st, rep from * ending last rep after 1st set of 2tr into next st, turn.

Row 2 forms pattern; repeat to required length.

materials

- 4mm hook
- Sublime Baby Cashmere Merino DK, Splash (A), Marmite (B), Vanilla (C), Ragdoll (D)

see other variations page 97

variation 1
Raspberry ripple Using yarn A, work as given for main pattern, changing to yarn D at the end of the row for stripe.

jasper

Main pattern: Using yarn F, ch22+4.

Row 1: 1tr into 6th ch from hook, ch1, sk1, 1tr into next ch, ch1, sk1, * 1tr into next 4ch, ch1 **, (sk1, 1tr into next, ch1) 3 times, sk1, rep from * to ** once more, sk1, 1tr into last ch, turn.

Row 2: ch4 (counts as 1tr and ch1), sk2, * 1tr into next 4sts, ch1, (sk1, 1tr into next st, ch1) 3 times, rep from * ending last rep with 1tr into ch3, turn.

Row 3: ch3 (counts as 1tr), sk1, * (1tr into next ch1sp, 1tr into next st) twice, 1tr into next ch1sp, ch1, sk1, 1tr into next st, ch1, 1tr into next st, rep from * once more, 1tr into next ch1sp, 1tr into top of ch3, turn.

Rows 2–3 form pattern; repeat to required length.

Alternatively, mirror Row 2 to set two rows, then work Row 3 and a mirroring row for a chunkier design.

Project notes: Coffeepot cosy.
Ch, multiples of 20 until ch fit around the pot. Work as main pattern, add a shell edge and button to fasten.

materials

- 5mm hook: main
- Rowan Kid Classic Lavender ice (F)
- 4mm hook: Var 1–5
- King Cole Bamboo Cotton DK in Yellow (A), Moss (B), Damson (C), Opal (D), Cobalt (E)

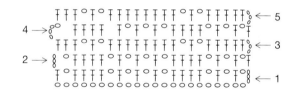

see other variations page 98

variation 1

Half treble crochet Using yarn C, ch20+2. Work as given for main pattern using htr throughout and ch2 for turning.

waffle

Main pattern: Using yarn A, ch21.

Row 1: tr into 4th ch from hook, tr into each ch to end, turn.

Row 2: ch3, * work 1tr around front post of next 2sts (FPtr), work 1tr into next st, rep from * to end, turn.

Row 3: ch3, * 1tr into first 2sts, * FPtr into next st, 1tr into next 2sts, rep from * to end, turn.

Rows 2–3 form pattern; repeat these rows until 11 rows have been worked. Fasten off.

materials

- 4mm hook: main, Var 1–4
- Sublime Baby Cashmere Merino Silk DK in Baby Pink (A), Beige (B), Green (C)
- 12mm hook: Var 5
- hoopla yarn

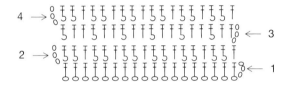

see other variations page 99

variation 1

Bumpy Work as given for main pattern, alternating between A and B yarns.

seaside

Notes: TRTOG=work a set of double crochet stitches together, over a number of stitches.

Main pattern: Using yarn A, ch27.

Row 1: tr3tog over 4th, 5th 6th ch from hook, * ch1, (1dtr into next ch, ch1) twice, (1dtr, ch1, 1dtr) into next st, (ch1, 1dtr into next ch,) twice, ch1, tr7tog over next 7sts, rep from * ending with tr4tog over last 4sts, turn.

Row 2: ch3, 1tr into 1st ch sp, * work (1tr into top of dtr, 1tr into ch sp) 5 times, 1tr into next dtr, work tr2tog over next 2 ch1sp's, rep from * ending last rep working tr2 tog over last ch sp and top of tr4tog, turn.

Row 3: ch3, sk1, 3trtog over next 3sts, * ch1, (1dtr in next st, ch1) twice, (1dtr, ch1, 1dtr) in next st, (ch1, 1dtr into next st) twice, ch1, tr7tog over next 7sts rep from * ending 4trtog over last 4sts, turn.

Rows 2–3 form the pattern; repeat to required length.

materials

- 4mm hook: main, Var 1, 2, 5
- Sublime Baby Cashmere Merino DK in Seasaw (A), Nutkin (B), Puffin (C), Pinkaboo (D)
- 12mm hook: Var 3
- blue and beige hoopla yarn
- 3mm hook: Var 4
- DCM Starlet (E)

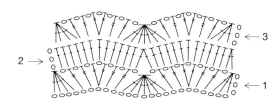

see other variations page 100

variation 1

Hoopla! Using 12mm hook and beige yarn, ch15+3 turning chain. Row 1: tr tog over 4th, 5th, 6th ch from hook, ch1, (1dtr into next ch, ch1) twice, (1dtr, ch1, 1dtr) into next ch, (ch1, 1dtr into next ch,) twice, ch1, tr4tog over last 4sts, turn. Fasten off yarn A and join in yarn B. Row 2: ch3, 1tr into 1st ch sp, work (1tr into top of dtr, 1tr into ch sp) 5 times, 1tr into next dtr, work tr2tog over next 2 ch1sps, tr2tog over last ch sp and top of tr4tog, turn. Row 3: ch3, sk1, 3trtog over next 3sts, ch1, (1dtr into next st, ch1) twice, (1dtr, ch1, 1dtr) in next st, (ch1, 1dtr into next st) twice, ch1, 4trtog over last 4sts, turn. Rows 2–3 form the pattern, work 2 rows in each colour to required length.

dot

Main pattern: Using yarn A, ch20.

Row 1: 1dc into 2nd ch from hook, * ch2, sk2, 1dc into next ch, rep from * to end, joining yarn B on last st, turn; do not break yarn A.

Row 2: using yarn B, ch4, * 3tr into ch2sp, ch1, rep from * to end, turn, do not break yarn B.

Row 3: return to beginning of Row 2, draw a through under 4th of 4ch, ch1 (counts as 1dc) * ch2, 1dc into ch1sp, rep form * to end, drawing yarn B through last st, turn.

Row 4: using yarn B, work as Row 2.

Rep Rows 3–4 throughout, always starting each row at the end that the correct colour was left.

Rows 3–4 form pattern; repeat these rows, working each row in correct colour.

materials

- 4 mm hook: main, Var 1-4
- Paton's DK cotton in White (A), Raffia (B), Orchard (C), Lilac (D), Foxglove (E), Denim (F), Nougat (G), Jade (H)
- 12mm hook: Var 5
- hoopla yarn

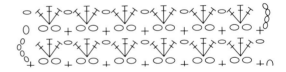

see other variations page 101

variation 1
Different coloured dots Work Rows 1 and 3 in alternating colours.

chain reaction

Notes: EXDC=extended double crochet.

Main pattern: using yarn A, ch17.

Row 1: 1exdc into 3rd ch from hook, 1exdc in each st to end, turn.

Row 2: ch1, 1dc into front loop of 1st exdc, * ch6, 1dc in front loop of next exdc, rep from * ending on 1dc in front of last exdc, turn.

Row 3: ch1, 1exdc in empty loop of 1st exdc, 1exdc in every empty loop of each exdc to end, turn.

Rows 2–3 form pattern; repeat to required length.

materials

- 4mm hook: main, Var1-3, 5
- Debbie Bliss Rialto in Baby Pink (A), Light Green (B), Brown (C), Emerald (D), Navy Blue (E)
- 12mm hook: Var 4
- hoopla yarn

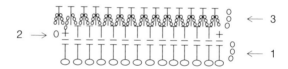

see other variations page 102.

variation 1

Colour variation Work as given for main pattern using yarn A for Rows 1–2 and yarn B for Rows 3–4, keeping working in stripe sequence as set.

annette

Main pattern: using yarn A, ch21+4 for turning.

Row 1: 1tr into 5th ch from hook. * ch1, sk1, 1tr into next ch, rep from * to end, turn.

Row 2: ch4 (counts as 1tr and ch), sk1 ch sp, 1tr into top of next st, rep from * working last tr into the top of tch, turn.

Row 2 forms pattern; repeat to required length.

materials

■ 5mm hook
■ Rowan Kid Classic in Lavender Ice (A), Tea Rose (B), Rosewood (C), Tattoo (D)

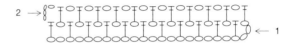

see other variations page 103

variation 1

Offset mesh Using yarn B, ch21+4 for turning. Row 1: work as Row 1 of main pattern. Row 2: ch5, sk 1st st, 1tr into 1st ch sp, * ch1, sk1, 1tr into next ch1 sp, rep from * to end, working last tr into top of tch, turn. Row 2 forms pattern; repeat Row 2 to required length.

bob

Notes: MB=make bobble. To make a bobble, work 4 open tr in same st leaving 5 loops on hook, draw yarn through all 5 loops.

Main pattern: using yarn A, ch23.

Row 1: 1dc into the 2nd ch from the hook, 1dc into each ch to end, turn (22sts).

Rows 2–4: ch1, 1dc into each st to end, turn.

Row 5: ch1, 1dc into each of next 3sts, *MB, 1 dc into each of next 4sts, rep from * 3 more times, 1dc into each of next 3sts.

Rows 2–5 form the bobble pattern. Repeat these rows until 4 sets of bobbles have been completed. Then repeat Rows 2–4 once more. Fasten off.

materials

- 4mm hook
- King Cole Bamboo Cotton in Aqua (A), Opal (B), Yellow (C), Rose (D), Moss (E), Plum (F)

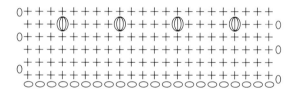

see other variations page 104

variation 1

Multi-coloured bobbles Using yarn A, work Rows 1–5 as given for main pattern, working 1st bobble in yarn C, 2nd bobble in yarn D, 3rd bobble in yarn E, 4th bobble in yarn F. Rows 6–8: work as Rows 2–4. Rep row 5 with coloured bobbles using picture as guide.

cables

Notes: FPDTR=front post dtr
BPDTR=back post dtr.
FPDTR3TOG=front post dtr 3
together.

Main pattern: Using yarn A, ch23.

Row 1: 1tr into 5th ch from hook
and each st to end, turn.

Row 2: ch3, sk1,1trc next 3sts, *
1BPdtr into next 4sts, 1trc into 4sts,
rep from * ending last rep with 1trc
to tch.

Row 3: ch3, sk1, 1trc into next 3sts,
work cable as follows, sk2, 1FPdtr
into next 2sts, work 1FPdtr into
each of the sk2 sts, (1st cable
worked), 1dtr into next 4sts, work
cable over next 4sts, 1dtrc into next
3sts and ch3, turn.

Row 4: ch3, sk1, 5trc, * 1BPdtr into
next 4sts, 1trc into next 4sts, rep
from * ending last rep with 1trc
into last 2sts and 1trc into dtr.

Row 5: ch3, sk1, 1trc into next 2sts,
* sk2, 1FPdtr into next 2sts, work
1FPdtr into each of the sk2 sts,
(1st cable worked), 1trc into next
4sts, rep from * once more, 1tr into
last 2sts, turn.

Rows 2–5 form pattern; repeat to
required length.

materials

- 4mm hook
- Debbie Bliss Rialto in
  Emerald (A), Bark (B),
  Light Green (C)

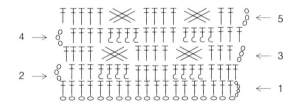

see other variations page 105

variation 1

Using yarn B, work Rows 1–3 as given for the main pattern, wrking a row of tr after eah
set of Rows 2–3 are completed.

basket weave

Main pattern: Using hoopla yarn and a 12mm hook, ch26.

Row 1: 1tr into the 4th ch from hook, 1tr into each ch to end, turn.

Rows 2–4: ch3, * 1FPtr into next 4sts, 1BPtr into next 4sts, rep from * twice more working last st around tch, turn.

Rows 5–7: ch3, * 1BPtr into next 4sts, 1FPtr into next 4sts, rep from * twice more working last st around tch, turn.

Rows 2–7 form pattern: repeat until 15 rows have been worked. Fasten off yarn.

materials

- 4mm hook: Var 1-5
- Sublime Baby Cashmere Merino in Lemon Yellow (A), Purple (B), Blue (C)
- 12mm hook: main
- hoopla yarn

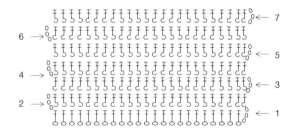

see other variations page 106

variation 1
Work as given for main pattern with Rows 1–4 in yarn A and Rows 5–7 in yarn B.

speckle

Notes: FPdtr = Front post dtr.

Main pattern: using yarn A, ch18.

Row 1: 1dc into 3rd ch from hook, 1dc in each st to end, turn.

Row 2: ch1, sk1, 1dc into each st, 1dc into tch, do not turn. Fasten off yarn A and join in yarn B.

Row 3: ch1, 1dc in each st to end, turn.

Row 4: work as Row 2. Do not break yarn B.

Row 5: return to beg of Row 4, join in yarn C, ch1, 1dc in each st to end, turn. Do not fasten off yarn C but join in yarn A.

Row 6: ch1, 1dc into next 2sts, * 1FPdtr into corresponding st of

Row 2, 1dc into each of next 2sts, rep from * to end.

Row 7: work as Row 2. Join in yarn C.

Row 8: ch1, 1dc in each st to end, turn. Do not break yarn C. Return to beg of Row 8, join in yarn B.

Row 9: ch1, 1dc into 1st st, * 1FPdtr into the FPdtr of Row 6, 1dc into each of next 2sts, rep from * to end.

materials

- 4mm hook
- Debbie Bliss Rialto in Brown (A), Spruce (B), Dark Navy (C), Sage (D), Baby Pink (E)

Row 10: work as Row 2.

Repeat Rows 5–10 once more. Fasten off.

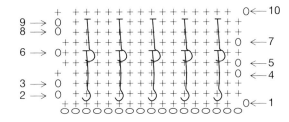

variation 1

see other variations on page 107

Piping Work as given for main pattern using yarns E, D and B work as main block with the following changes.

Row 6: instead of working into the corresponding st of Row 2, work into the 5th st of Row 2, work next FPdtr into the 2nd st along from that, rep along the row.

Row 12: ch1, 1dc, then work FPdtr into the previous FPdtr as before and 3dc at the end.

solomon's knot

Main pattern: using yarn A, ch2.

Row 1: * draw up loop 2.5 cm (1 inch), work 1dc through back strand of elongated loop just made, rep from * for 5 more times. This forms the foundation row.

Row 2: work 2 extra elongated loops to turn, work 1dc in centre of 4th dc or knot from hook, * (draw loop up 6mm (¼ inch), work 1dc in back strand of same loop) twice, sk1 knot and work 1dc in 2nd knot, rep from * across row and end with 1dc in last st.

Row 2 forms the pattern; repeat to required length.

materials

- 3mm hook: main, Var 2, 4, 5
- Debbie Bliss Rialto in Emerald (A), Brown (B), Spruce (C), Charisma Mohair (D), DMC Starlet (E)
- 12mm hook: Var 3
- hoopla yarn (F)

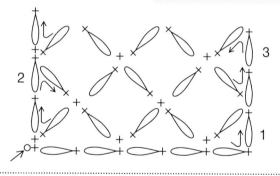

variation 1

see other variations on page 108

Little Solomon Using yarn B, work as given for main pattern but keep loops 1.25cm (½ inch) long.

the wall

Main pattern: using yarn A, ch15+1 for turning.

Row 1: 1dc into 2nd ch from hook, 1dc into every ch to end, turn.

Row 2: ch1, work 1dc into the back loop of each st to end, creating rib effect, turn.

Row 3: ch1 (counts as first dc), sk1, 1dc into back loop of next 3 sts.   * Work 1sp st into st 2 rows below, 1dc into back loop of next 3sts, rep from * to end, turn.

Row 4: work as Row 2.

Row 5: ch1 (counts as first dc), sk1, 1dc into back of next st, * 1sp st into 2 rows below, 1dc into back loop of next 3sts. Repeat from * twice more, 1sp stitch 2 rows below in next st, 1dc into back loop of last st, turn.

Repeat Rows 2–5 to form the pattern.

materials

- 4mm hook
- Debbie Bliss Rialto DK in Gold (A), Earth (B), Duck Egg (C), Scarlet (D), Forest (E)

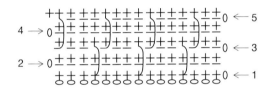

variation 1

see other variations on page 109

Breeze blocks Using yarn B, ch15+1 for turning. **Row 1:** work as Row 1 of main pattern. Fasten off yarn B and join in yarn C. **Row 2:** ch2, 1htr into back loops of each st to end, turn. **Row 3:** ch2, sk1, 1htr into each st to end, turn. Drop yarn C, but do not cut. **Row 4:** join in yarn B, ch1, 1dc into front loop of each st to end, turn. **Row 5:** ch1, sk1 (counts as 1dc), 1dc in front loop of next 3sts, work 1trtr in front of stitch 4 rows below, 1dc in front loop of next 4sts, 1trtr in front post of the next stitch, 4 rows below, 1dc in the front loop of the last 4sts, drop yarn B, turn. **Row 6:** join in yarn C, ch2, sk1, 1htr in back loop of each st to end, turn. **Row 7:** ch2, sk1, 1htr in each stitch to end, drop yarn C, turn. **Row 8:** repeat Row 4. **Row 9:** ch1, sk1 (counts as 1dc), 1dc in front loop of next 2 sts, * work 1trtr in front of stitch 4 rows below, 1dc in front loop of next 4sts, rep from * once more, 1trtr in front post of the next stitch 4 rows below, 1dc into each st to end, drop yarn B, turn. Repeat pattern using the picture as a guide.

starry-eyed

Main pattern: using yarn A, ch24.

Row 1: 1tr into 8th ch from hook to create corner loop, (ch1, 1tr) 3 times into same ch, * skip ch3, 1tr into next ch, (ch1, 1tr) 3 times into same st (1 shell has been worked), rep from * to last ch4, sk3, 1tr into last ch, turn.

Row 2: ch3, * 1tr into middle of shell, (ch1, 1tr) 3 times into same ch sp, rep from * to last st, 1tr into middle of corner loop space, turn.

Row 2 forms the pattern. Repeat to required length.

materials

- 4mm hook
- Sublime Extra Fine Merino Wool DK in Splash (A), Vanilla (B), Salty Grey (C), Piglet (D)

variation 1

see other variations on page 110

Colour variation Work as given for main pattern, working Row 1 in yarn A, Row 2 in yarn B, Row 3 in yarn C. Repeat stripe to required length.

harlequin

Main pattern: using yarn A, ch21+1 for turning.

Row 1: 1dc into 2nd ch from hook, 1dc into next st, * sk3, 7tr into next st, sk3, 1dc into each of the next 3ch, rep from * once more, 1dc into last 2sts, turn.

Row 2: ch2, tr4tog over the next 4sts, ch3, 1dc into each of the next 3sts, ch3, tr7tog over the next 7sts, ch3, 1dc into each of the next 3sts, ch3, tr4tog over the last 4sts, turn.

Row 3: ch2, 4tr into top of tr4tog, sk ch3, 1dc into each of the next 3sts, sk ch3, 7tr into top of

tr7tog, sk ch3, 1dc into each of the next 3sts, sk ch3, 4tr into top of tr4tog, turn.

Row 4: ch1, 1dc into each of the first 2sts, * ch3, tr7tog over next 7sts, ch3, 1dc into each of the next 3sts, rep from * once more, ch3, 1dc into last 2sts, turn.

Rows 2–4 form the pattern; repeat to required length.

Project notes: Cowl. Using Rowan Big Wool and a 10mm hook, ch61. Work as per main pattern. Stitch short ends together with a darning needle.

materials

- ◾ 4mm hook
- ◾ King Cole Bamboo Cotton DK in Damson (A), Blush (B), Aqua (C), Cobalt (D), Oyster (E), Opal (F)

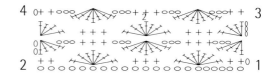

variation 1

see other variations on page 111

Circle effect Work as given for main pattern using yarn A for Row 1, yarn B for Rows 2–3, and yarn A for Row 4.

crocodile

Main pattern: using yarn A, ch18.

Row 1: 1tr into 3rd ch from hook. *
Ch2, sk2, 2tr into next ch. Repeat
from * to end. Turn work
anti-clockwise.

Row 2: working along edge, ch1,
5trs around the first tr post of Row
1. Turn work again and work 5trs
into the second tr post. Ss in
between next 2trs to complete the
"scale." * Ch2, and work 5trs into the
next tr of the next pair of trs. Insert
hook from right to left-fold over the
chain to easily work the next scale,
or turn piece as you work to place
the stitches in a shell shape. Work
5trs into other tr, completing the
scale. Ss in between next 2trs to join.
Repeat from * to end.

Row 3: ch1, ss into middle of scale.
Ch3, 1tr into same st. * Ch2, sk2,
2trs into ch sp between scales, ch2,

sk2, 2trs into centre of next scale.
Repeat from * to final scale.

Row 4: ch1, sk 2tr, work scale into
next pair of trs. Skip next 2trs, work
scale into alternate pairs of tr, ss in
between last 2.

Ch3, 1tr into same st to begin next
row, repeating Row 3 to continue
the process. Work the crocodile
scales into alternate pairs of trs.

materials

- 4mm hook
- Debbie Bliss Rialto DK in
  Dark Green (A), Earth (B),
  Gold (C), Apple (D), Scarlet
  (E), Grey (F), Teal (G)

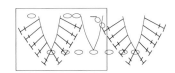

....

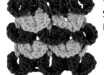

variation 1

see other variations on page 112

Speckled crocodile Work as given for main pattern, working Rows 1–2 in yarn A and
Rows 3–4 in yarn C.

bullion

Notes: BS=wrap the yarn 7 times around the hook, insert the hook into the next ch sp, pull through a loop, wrap the yarn again and pull through all the loops on the hook.

Main pattern: using yarn A, ch17.

Row 1: 1dc in 2nd ch from hook, 1tr in each st to end, turn.

Row 2: ch3, sk1, 1tr into each of next 4sts, * 1BS in next st, 1tr in each of next 5 sts, rep from * to end, working last tr into top of tch, turn.

Row 3: ch1, sk1, 1dc into each st, 1dc into top of tch, turn.

Row 4: ch3, sk1, 1tr into next st, * 1BS in next st, 1tr into each of next 5 st, rep from * to end, working last tr into top of tch, turn.

Row 5: work as Row 3.

Row 6: work as Row 2.

Row 7: wok as Row 3.

Row 8: work as Row 4.

Row 9: repeat Row 3.

materials

- 4mm hook
- Debbie Bliss Cotton in Purple (A), Teal Blue (B)

Row 10: work as Row 2.

Row 11: work as Row 3. Fasten off.

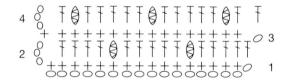

variation 1

see other variations on page 113

Colour stripe Work as given for main pattern, working every odd row in yarn A and every even row in yarn B. Continue working in stripes as set.

curlicues

Main pattern: using yarn A, ch17.

Row 1: 1tr into 4th ch from hook, 1tr in each st to end, turn.

Row 2: ch3, 1tr into each st to end, turn.

Row 3: ch3, 1tr into each of next 4sts, * ch10, 2tr in 4th ch from hook, 3tr in each of next ch6 (1st curlicues worked), ss in top of last tr worked in main fabric, 1tr in each of next 5sts, rep from * to end, turn.

Row 4: repeat Row 2.

Row 5: ch3, 1tr into each of next 2sts, * ch10, 2tr in 4th ch from hook, 3tr in each of next 6sts, ss in top of last tr worked in main fabric, 1tr in each of next 5sts, rep from * to end, omitting last 3tr of final rep, turn.

Repeat Rows 2–5, ending with a row of tr.

materials

- 4mm hook
- Sublime Baby Cashmere Merino DK in Ragdoll (A), Piglet (B), Puzzle (C), Cuddle (D), Little Miss Plum (E)

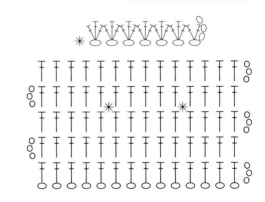

variation 1

Colour variation Work as given for main pattern using yarn B for curlicues.

see other variations on page 114

trellis

Main pattern: using yarn A, ch24.

Row 1: 1tr in 4th ch from hook,
* sk1, 1ch, 1tr in next ch, rep from *
to end, turn.

Row 2: ch4, sk 1st st * 1tr into ch1
worked in between trs, 1ch, rep
from * to end, working last tr into
top of tch, turn.

Row 2 forms pattern; repeat to
required length.

materials

- 4mm hook
- Debbie Bliss Rialto in Sage
  (A), Baby Pink (B), Grey (C)

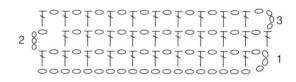

see other variations on page 115

variation 1

Colour variation Work as given for main pattern: Rows 1–3 in yarn A, Rows 4–6 in yarn B
and Rows 7–9 in yarn C.

daisy chain

Main pattern: In the yarn at right, chain 25 (multiples of 8+4).

Row 1: into 8th ch from hook, work * 3dtr cl, ch7, 3dtr cl into same st. Ch3, sk3, 1dc into next st. Ch3, sk3. * Rep from * to * along ch to end, ending in dc. Turn.

Row 2: ch3, work 3dtr cl into ch sp (petal made). Ch3, and work 2dtr cl into top of petal. Ch3, ** 1dc into next ch sp. Begin to make 2dtr cl into same st, leaving 3 loops on the hook. Begin making 3dtr cluster into next ch sp, keeping 3 loops on the hook. Begin to make 3dtr cl into next st, leaving 3 loops on hook, YOH, draw loop through all 9 loops on hook. Ch3, make 2dtr cl into top of st just made. ** Repeat from ** to ** along to end, finishing with 1dc into ch sp, ch3, begin 2dtr

cl, begin 3dtr cl into next ch sp, YOH, draw through 6 loops. Turn.

Row 3: ch3, 2dtr cl into first st. Ch3, sk ch-3 sp, 1dc into next st, ch3. Repeat from * to * along, working the 3dtr cl, ch7, 3dtr into the centre of the flower made on previous row. End with 3dtr cl into the very last st. Turn.

Row 4: ch7, begin 2dtr cl into 4th ch from hook, leaving 3 loops on hook. Begin making 3dtr cl into each of the next 2ch sps, YOH draw through 9 loops. Ch3, make 2dtr cl into same st. Repeat from ** to ** to end, ending with dc into turning ch, turn.

Row 5: ch3, rep from * into top of next flower, to * across each ch3 sp.

materials

■ 4mm hook
■ King Cole Bamboo Cotton DK in Red (A), Blush (B)

Repeat Rows 2–5.

see other variations on page 116

variation 1

Simple petal stitch Ch30 (multiples of 6). **Row 1:** working in 6th ch from hook, begin working a 2dtr cl, leaving 3 loops on the hook. Sk5 ch, begin 3dtr cl leaving 3 loops on the hook. YOH, draw loop through all 6 loops. * Ch4, begin 2dtr cl into top of cl, leaving 3 loops on the hook. Begin 3dtr cl into same ch as petal below, sk 5. Begin 3dtr cl into next. YOH, draw through all 9 loops. Rep from * to end, just working 2 petals into last ch. Turn. **Row 2:** ch4, 2dtr cl into first st. Ch4, begin 2dtr cluster into top of cl. Begin 3dtr cl into first flower centre. Begin 3dtr cl into next flower centre. YOH, draw through all 9 loops. Rep from * working sts into flower centres instead of ch, repeat to end, working 2 petals into last. Turn.

peacock

Main pattern: using yarn A, ch21+1.

Row 1: 1dc in 2nd ch from hook, * sk4, 9dtr into next st, sk4, 1dc into next, rep from * to end, turn.

Row 2: ch4, 1dtr into 1st dc, * sk4, 1dc into next st (centre of 9 dtr), ch3, sk4, work (1dtr, 1ch, 1dtr) into next st, rep from * to end, 2dtr into last st, turn.

Row 3: ch1, 1dc in between 2 dtr, * sk1, ch3, 9dtr into next st, sk ch3, 1dc into 1ch in between next 2dtr, rep from * to end, dc into top of tch, turn.

Rows 2–3 form the pattern; repeat to required length.

materials

- 4mm hook
- King Cole Bamboo Cotton DK in Peacock (A), Yellow (B), Damson (C), Moss (D) Aqua (E), Blush (F)

---

see other variations on page 117

variation 1

Large-scale simple peacock stitch Using yarn A, ch28+1. **Row 1:** 1dc in 2nd ch from hook, * sk6, 13Etr (extended double crochet) into next st, sk6, 1dc into next, rep from * to end, turn. **Row 2:** ch4, 1Etr into dc, * ch5, 1dc into 7th Etr, ch5 (1Etr, 1ch, 1Etr) into dc, rep from * ending last rep working 2Etr into last st, turn. **Row 3:** ch1, 1dc in between 1st 2Etr, sk5ch, 13Etr into next dc, sk5ch, 1dc into 1ch in between next 2Etr, rep from * ending last rep working 1dc into last st, turn. Rows 2–3 form the pattern; repeat to required length.

fruit punch

Main pattern: using yarn A, ch15+3 for turning ch.

Row 1: work into 4th ch from hook as follows: * (YOH, draw loop through ch leaving loops on hook) 4 times, YOH and draw through 8 loops, YOH and draw through 2 loops (1 pineapple made), ch1, sk1, rep from * ending last rep with 1tr into last ch.

Row 2: ch3, 1 pineapple into 1st ch sp,* ch1, 1 pineapple into next ch sp, rep from * to end, 1tr into dtrc, turn.

Row 2 forms the pattern; repeat to required length.

materials

- 4mm hook
- King Cole Bamboo Cotton in Yellow (A), Moss (B), Oyster (C), Damson (D), Red (E)

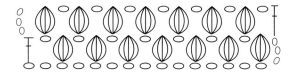

see other variations on page 118

variation 1

Pineapples with leaves Work alternate rows in yarns A and B for a leafy pineapple effect, using the picture as a guide.

stand out

Main pattern (heart design):
using yarn A, ch24+4.

Row 1: 1tr into 5th ch from hook
(counts as 1tr and ch1), * ch1, sk1,
1tr into next, rep from * to end,
turn.

Rows 2–10: work from chart. Each
square represents 2sts. Work
coloured blocks as 1tr into either
the ch sp or stitch below. Work ch4
at the beg of each row.

materials

▓ 4mm hook
▓ King Cole Cotton Bamboo
   DK in Opal (A), Red (B),
   Star (C), Cobalt (D), Moss
   (E), Yellow (F)

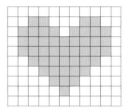

see other variations on page 119

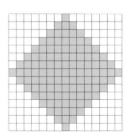

variation 1

Diamond square Using yarn B, ch30+4. **Row 1:**
1tr into 5th ch from hook (counts as 1tr and
ch1), * ch1, sk1, 1tr into next, rep from * to end,
turn. **Rows 2–15:** work from chart.

broomstick lace

Notes: YOH=yarn over hook. EBS=extended broomstick stitch. To work an EBS, insert hook into yarn, YOH, pull loop through, YOH, pull loop through, lengthen loop and slip onto knitting needle.

Main pattern: using yarn A, ch20.

Row 1: lengthen the loop on hook and slip it onto big knitting needle. Hold needle in your left hand, * insert the hook into the next ch, YOH, draw the loop through and place on needle, rep from * to end, and do not turn.

Row 2: slip first 5sts off the needle and onto the hook from right to left, YOH, draw through all 5 loops, work 5dc through the 5 loops, * slip next 5 loops into hook from right to left, YOH and draw through 2 loops, work a further 4dc onto the loops, rep from * twice more, do not turn.

Rows 1–2 form the pattern. Repeat to required length.

materials

- 4mm hook
- 12mm knitting needle,
- King Cole Bamboo Cotton in Cream (A), Cobalt (B), Yellow (C), Charisma Mohair (D)

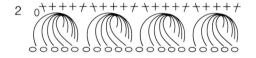

see other variations on page 120

variation 1

Broomstick clusters Using yarn B, ch23. **Row 1:** 1dc into 2nd ch from hook, 1dc in to each ch to end, do not turn. **Row 2:** work as Row 1 of main pattern. **Row 3:** slip 1st st onto hook, YOH, and pull through 1st loop. Insert hook under separate thread leading to new loop, YOH, pull through 2 loops, ch2, * slip next 5 loops onto the hook from right to left, ch4, rep from * twice more, ch2, slip 1st st onto hook, 1dc into last loop, turn. **Row 4:** ch1, 1dc into each st to end, turn. **Row 5:** as Row 4, but do not turn. Repeat Rows 2–5.

tunisian crochet

Main pattern: using yarn A, ch15, then begin Tunisian simple stitch (TSS).

Row 1 (forwards): insert hook into 2nd ch from hook, YOH, and pull loop through, keep loop on hook, * insert into next ch, YOH, and pull loop through, keep loop on hook, rep from *, keeping all loops on hook. Do not turn.

Row 1 (return): YOH and pull through 1 loop, * YOH and pull through 2 loops, rep from * until 1 loop remains on hook.

Row 2 (forwards): * insert hook from side to side under next vertical bar, YOH, and draw loop through, rep from * keeping all loops on hook.

Row 2 (return): work as Row 1.

Row 2 forms the pattern; repeat to required length.

materials

- 4mm hook
- Sublime Baby Cashmere Merino in Pinkaboo (A), Caterpillar (B), Little Miss Plum (C), Teddy Red (D), Puffin (E)

see other variations on page 121

variation 1

Colour variation Work as given for main pattern, working Row 1 in yarn A and Row 2 in yarn B. Repeat Row 2, keeping the stripe sequence correct.

more tunisian crochet

Main pattern: using A, ch15 then begin Tunisian knit stitch (TKS).

Row 1 (forwards): insert hook into first chain space from hook, YOH and pull loop through, keep loop on hook * insert into next ch, YOH and pull loop through, rep from * keeping all loops on hook. Do not turn.

Row 1 (return): YOH and pull through 1 loop, * YOH and pull through 2 loops. Repeat from * until 1 loop remains on hook.

Row 2 (forwards): * insert hook in next stitch between the 2 vertical bars and under the horizontal bars, from front to back through the fabric, YOH and pull up a loop, rep from * to end.

Row 2 (return): work as Row 1 return.

Row 2 forms the pattern; repeat to required length.

materials

- 4mm hook
- Patons Double Knit Cotton in Orchard (A), Lilac (B), Denim (C), Raffia (D)

see other variations on page 122

variation 1

Simple lace Work Row 1 as given for main pattern using yarn B and ch16. **Row 2 (forwards):** ch1, * sk1, insert hook under next YOH and pull loop through, ch1, rep from * to end, keeping all loops on hook. **Row 2 (return):** work as Row 1 return of main pattern. Row 2 forms the pattern; repeat to required length.

variations

solid weave

see base design on page 31

variation 2

Half treble crochet Using yarn C, ch22.
Row 1: 1htr into 3rd ch from hook, 1htr into
each ch to end, turn (20sts). **Row 2:** ch2,
1htr into first st, 1htr into each st to end,
turn. Repeat Row 2 a further 16 times.

variation 4

Two-row stripe Work as given for main
pattern: Rows 1–2 in yarn A and Rows 3–4 in
yarn B. Repeat Rows 1–4 to required length.

variation 3

Double treble crochet Using yarn D, ch25.
Row 1: 1dtr into 5th ch from hook, 1 dtr into
each ch to end (20sts). **Row 2:** ch5, 1dtr into
first st, 1dtr into each st to end, turn. Repeat
Row 2 a further 7 times.

variation 5

Double crochet Using hoopla yarn, ch9.
Row 1: 1dc into 2nd ch from hook, 1dc
into each ch to end, turn (8 sts). **Row 2:** ch1,
1dc into each st to end. Repeat Row 2 to
required length.

shelley

see base design on page 32

variation 2
Beaded Work as given for main pattern using yarn B. Thread beads onto your yarn before starting and add in the beads as you crochet.

variation 3
Rough Work as given for main pattern, but use raffia instead of yarn. This results in a wonderful texture.

variation 4
Diagonal stripes Work as given for main pattern using yarn B and yarn C as follows. **Row 1:** work as main pattern. **Row 2:** 1st full shell in yarn C. **Row 3:** 3rd full shell in yarn C. **Row 4:** 2nd full shell in yarn C. **Row 5:** 2nd full shell in yarn C. Keeping pattern as set, moving coloured shell over 1 each row.

variation 5
Surf Using yarn A, ch28. **Row 1:** 1tr into the 4th ch from hook, ch2, 2tr into same st. * sk3, (2tr, 2ch, 2tr) into next ch, rep from * to end, turn. **Row 2:** ch3, 1tr into the 1st st, (2tr, 2ch, 2tr) into ch2sp, rep from * to end, turn. Row 2 forms the pattern. Repeat to required length.

variations

ribbed and ridged

see base design on page 35

variation 2

Aligned Using yarn C, work as given for main pattern for Row 1. On Row 2, work 1st st into back loop and 2nd st into front loop, and keep alternating between back and front loops to end. Row 2 forms the pattern; repeat to required length.

variation 4

Double crochet Using yarn E, ch22. **Row 1:** 1dc into 3rd ch from hook, 1dc into each ch to end. **Row 2:** ch1, 1dc into back loop of 1st st, 1dc into back loop of each st to end, 1dc into top of tch, turn. Row 2 forms the pattern; repeat to required length.

variation 3

Double treble crochet Using yarn D, ch24. **Row 1:** 1dtr into 5th ch from hook, 1dtr into each ch to end, turn. **Row 2:** ch4, 1dtr into back loop of 1st st, 1dtr into back loop of each st to end, 1dtr into top of tch, turn. Row 2 forms the pattern. Repeat to required length.

variation 5

Colour variation Work as given for main pattern, changing colour on every 2nd row.

fan stitch

see base design on page 36

variation 2

Four-colour stripe Work as given for main pattern, in a single row stripe using colours A, B, C and D for 10 rows.

variation 4

Half treble crochet Using yarn A, ch21. Work as given for main pattern, working each fan using htr throughout and ch2 for turning on even rows.

variation 3

Triple treble crochet Using yarn D, ch21. Work as given for main pattern, working each fan using trtr throughout and ch5 for turning on even rows.

variation 5

Hoopla yarn Work as main block, but with hoopla yarn and a 10mm crochet hook.

variations

dorothy

see base design on page 39

variation 2
Textured crossed tr Using yarn E, work Row 1 as given for main pattern. **Row 2:** ch3, sk2, * 1tr into next st, 1tr into the skipped stitch, going BEHIND the tr, then inserting the hook from front to back around stem of stitch, sk1, rep from * to end, working 1tr into last st.

variation 3
Treble double cross Using yarn B, work Row 1 as given for main pattern. **Row 2:** ch2, sk2, * 1dc into next st, 1tr into next st, sk1, rep from * to end, turn. Row 2 forms the pattern; repeat to required length.

variation 4
Crossed double treble crochet Using yarn D, work Row 1 as given for main pattern. **Row 2:** ch4, sk2, 1dtr into next st, then work as per main pattern, using dtr instead of tr, with ch4 for turning at the beg of next row.

variation 5
Textured crossed double treble crochet Using yarn F, work as given for Variation 3, using dtr throughout and ch4 for turning.

ripples and waves

see base design on page 40

variation 2

Squared effect Using yarn C ch28+3. Work Row 1 as given for main pattern. **Row 2:** ch1, (1dc into 1st 2sts), * (1htr into next 2sts), (1tr into next 2sts), (1dtr into next 2sts), (1tr into next 2sts), (1htr into next 2sts), (1dc into next 2sts), rep from * to end. **Row 3:** work as Row 2 of main pattern. Rows 2-3 form the pattern; repeat to required length.

variation 4

Ribbed effect Using yarn D, work as given for main pattern for Row 1, then for Row 2, work as per main pattern but working into the back loop of each st.

variation 3

Double crochet Using yarn B, work as given for main pattern working in dc throughout and using ch1 for turning.

variations

jasper

see base design on page 43

variation 2

Blocked rows Using yarn B, ch20+4. **Row 1:** 1tr into 4th ch from hook, 1tr into each ch to end, turn. **Row 2:** ch4, sk2, 1tr into next st, * ch1, sk1, 1tr into next st, rep from * to end, working last tr into ch1, turn. **Row 3:** ch3, sk1, 1tr into each st to end, turn. Rows 2–3 form the pattern; repeat to required length.

variation 3

Lacy filet Using yarn C, ch20+3. **Row 1:** 1tr into 4th ch from hook, 1tr into next ch4, * ch1, sk1, 1tr into next ch, rep from * twice more, 1tr into next ch5, repeat from * twice, turn. **Row 2:** ch4, sk2, 1tr into next st, rep from * once, ch4, sk4, 1tr into next st, rep from * 3 times, ch4, 1tr into top of ch3, turn. **Row 3:** ch3, 4tr into ch loop,1tr into top of next st, rep from * 3 more times, 4tr into next ch loop, 1tr into top of next st rep from * twice more, turn. Rows 2–3 form the pattern. Repeat to required length.

variation 4

Mirrored filet Using yarn D, ch 20+2. **Row 1:** ch1, 1dc into each ch to end, turn. **Row 2:** ch4, sk1, 1tr into next 3sts, (ch1, sk1, 1tr into next st) 3 times, 1tr into next 4sts, (ch1, sk1, 1tr into next st) 3 times, turn. **Row3:** ch4, sk1, 1tr into next 3sts, (ch1, sk1, 1tr into next st) 3 times, 1tr into next 4sts, (ch1, sk1, 1tr into next st) 3 times, turn. Rows 2–3 form pattern; repeat to required length.

variation 5

Fences Using yarn F, ch20+2. **Row1:** 1tr into 4th ch from hook, 1tr in next ch3, * ch2, sk2, 1tr into next ch, rep from * once more, 1tr in next 4sts, repeat from * twice more. **Row 2:** as Row 1 working into sts and ch3sps. Row 2 forms the pattern; repeat to required length.

variations

waffle

see base design on page 44

variation 2
Texture Using yarn C, ch22. Work as per main pattern, using dtr throughout and ch4 for turning.

variation 3
Flow Work as given for Variation 2, alternating between B and C yarns.

variation 4
Double waffle Using yarn C, ch22. **Row 1:** 1tr into 4th ch from hook, 1tr into each ch to end, turn. **Row 2:** ch3, sk 1st st, 1tr into next st, * 1FPtr into each of the next 2sts, 1tr into next 2sts, rep from * ending last rep with 1tr into last st, turn. Row 2 forms the pattern. Repeat until 13 rows have been worked.

variation 5
Hoopla yarn Work as given for main pattern, starting with ch12.

seaside

see base design on page 47

variation 2
Striped colour Work as given for main pattern, working Rows 1, 3, 5 and 9 in yarn A and Rows 2, 4, 6 and 8 in yarn B.

variation 4
Sparkly Using 3mm hook, work as given for main pattern using yarn C.

variation 3
Sand, sea and sky Using the picture as a guide for colours, work as given for main pattern.

variation 5
Sequins Thread sequins onto your yarn and work as given for main pattern, adding sequins as desired.

dot

see base design on page 48

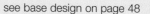

variation 2
Double treble crochet Using yarn A, work as given for main pattern, using dtr throughout and ch4 for turning.

variation 4
Stripy Work as per main pattern, working odd rows in colour A and every 2nd even row alternating between yarns F, E and C.

variation 3
More ch between dots Using yarn A for odd rows and yarn C for even rows work as follows: on Rows 1 and 3, work from * ch4, sk4 to spread dots out along the rows.

variation 5
Hoopla yarn Work as given for main pattern, using 12mm hook and hoopla yarn.

variations

chain reaction

see base design on page 51

variation 2
Lightweight chain Row 1: using yarn D, work as Row 1 of main pattern. **Row 2:** ch1, 1dc into front loop of 1st st, * ch6, 1dc into front loop of next 2sts, rep from * to end.

variation 4
Hoopla yarn Using 12mm hook, work as given for main pattern with hoopla yarn.

variation 3
Chained up Using E, work as per Variation 2. **Rows 1–2:** as per main pattern. **Row 3:** ch3, 1tr into empty loop of each st to end. **Row 4:** ch1, 1dc into front loop of 1st 2sts, * ch6, 1dc into front loop of next st, rep from * to end, turn. **Row 5:** ch3, 1exdc into empty loop of each st to end, turn. Rows 2–5 form the pattern; repeat to required length.

variation 5
Aligned chain loops Work Row 1 as given for main pattern using yarn B. **Row 2:** ch1, 1dc into front loop of 1st exdc, * ch6, 1dc in front loop of next 3 exdc, rep from * to end, turn. **Row 3:** ch1, 1exdc in empty loop of 1st st, 1exdc into each st to end, turn. Rows 2–3 form the pattern; repeat to required length.

annette

see base design on page 52

variation 2

Half treble crochet Using yarn A, ch20+3 for turning. **Row 1:** 1htr into 4th ch from hook * ch1, sk1, 1htr into next ch, rep from * to end, turn. **Row 2:** ch3, sk1 st ch sp, 1htr into top of next st, rep from * working last st into the top of tch, turn. Row 2 forms the pattern; repeat to required length.

variation 3

Double treble crochet Using yarn C, ch21+5 for turning. **Row 1:** 1dtr into 6th ch from hook, * ch1, sk1, 1dtr into next ch, rep from * to end, turn. **Row 2:** ch5, sk ch sp, 1dtr into top of next st, rep from * working last st into the top of tch, turn. Row 2 forms the pattern; repeat to required length.

variation 4

Triple treble Using yarn D, ch21+6 for turning. **Row 1:** 1dtr into 7th ch from hook, * ch1, sk1, 1trtr into next ch, rep from * to end, turn. **Row 2:** ch6, sk ch sp, 1trtr into top of next st, rep from * working last st into the top of tch, turn.

variation 5

Combining stitches Using yarn C, ch20+3.
Row 1: work in htr as given in Variation 2.
Row 2: ch4, then work as given using tr.
Row 3: ch5, then work as given using dtr.
Row 4: ch6, then work as given using trtr.
Row 5: work as Row 3. **Row 6:** work as Row 2. **Row 7:** ch3, then work as given using htr.

variations

bob

see base design on page 55

variation 2

Alternate bobbles Using yarn E, work Rows 1–5 as given for main pattern, working all bobbles in yarn D. **Rows 6–8:** work as Rows 2–4. **Row 9:** ch1, 1dc into next 6 sts, * MB, 1dc into each of next 4 sts, rep from * twice more, 1dc into last st, turn. Repeat from Row 2 until 5 sets of bobbles have been worked. Work Rows 2–4. Fasten off.

variation 3

Striped bobbles Work as given for main pattern, working Rows 1–4 in yarn F and Row 5 in yarn C, alternating between colours using the picture as a guide.

variation 4

Four-corner bobbles Work Rows 1–4 as given for main pattern in yarn C. **Row 5:** 1dc into each of the next 3st, MB, * 1dc into each of next 4sts, MB, dc into each st to end, turn. **Rows 6–8:** work as Rows 2–4 of main pattern. **Row 9:** work as Row 5. **Rows 10–12:** work as Rows 2–4 of main pattern. **Row 13:** work a 1dc into each of the next 13 sts, MB, 1dc into each of next 4 sts, MB, 1dc into each of the last 3st. **Rows 14–16:** rep Rows 2–4 of main block. **Row 17:** rep Row 13. **Rows 18–20:** rep Rows 2–4 of main block. Fasten off.

variation 5

Half and half bobbles Work as given for main pattern for Rows 2–5 twice, then Rows 2–4. Change to yarn D and work next row as follows: ch3, 1tr into the 4th st from the hook, 1tr into every st to end. Repeat last row 3 more times.

cables

see base design on page 56

variation 2

Big cable Using yarn C, work as given for main pattern. **Row 2:** ch3, sk1, 1tr in next 5sts, sk4, work 4FPdtr into next 4sts, work FPdtr in each of the sk4sts, 1tr into each st and tch, turn. **Row 3:** ch3, sk1, 1tr into each st to end, turn. Rows 2–3 form the pattern; repeat to required length.

variation 3
Off-set cable

Using yarn A, work Rows 1–3 as given for main pattern. **Row 4:** ch3, sk1, 1tr in next 5sts, * 1BPdtr in next 4sts, 1tr in next 4sts, rep from * ending last rep with 1tr into last 2sts and dtrc. **Row 5:** ch3, sk1, 1tr into next 2sts, * work cable over next 4sts, 1tr into next 4sts, rep from * once more, 1tr into last st and tch, turn. Repeat Rows 2–5 to form the pattern; repeat once more. Fasten off.

variation 4

Bobbles Using yarn B, ch25. **Row 1:** 1tr in 4th ch from hook, 1tr in each st to end, turn. **Row 2:** ch3, * 1tr into next 2sts, sk1, FPdtr3tog in next st on prev row, 1tr in top of same st, rep from * to last 2sts, 1tr into last 2sts, turn. **Row 3:** ch3, 1tr into each st to end, turn. Rows 2 and 3 form the pattern. Repeat 4 more times.

variation 5

Colour variation Work as given for main pattern, working Row 1 in yarn A, Row 2 in yarn B and Row 3 in yarn C. Repeat stripe pattern throughout.

basket weave

see base design on page 59

variation 2

Hoopla yarn Ch10. Work as given for main pattern, working Rows 2–7 once.

variation 3

Big basket weave Using yarn B, ch26. **Row1:** 1tr into 4th ch from hook, 1tr into each ch to end, turn. **Rows 2–9:** ch3, 1FPtr into 1st 12sts, 1BPtr into next 12 sts, working last st around tch, turn. **Rows 10–18:** ch3, * 1BPtr into first 12sts, 1FPtr into next 12sts, working last st around tch, turn.

variation 4

Little basket weave
Using yarn C, ch26.
Row 1: 1tr into 4th ch from hook, 1tr into each ch to end, turn. **Rows 2–3:** ch3, *1FPtr into next 2sts, 1BPtr into next 2sts, rep from * to end working last st around tch, turn. **Rows 4–5:** ch3, * 1BPtr into next 2sts, 1FPtr into next 2sts, rep from * to end working last st around tch, turn. Rows 2–5 form the pattern. Repeat until 28 rows have been worked. Fasten off yarn.

variation 5

Double treble crochet Using yarn A, ch17. **Row 1:** 1dtr into 5th ch from hook, 1dtr into each ch to end, turn. **Row 2:** ch4, *1FPtr into next 2sts, 1BPtr into next 2sts, rep from * to end, working last st around tch, turn. **Row 3:** ch4, * 1BPtr into next 2sts, 1FPtr into next 2sts, rep from * to end, working last st around tch, turn. Rows 2–3 form the pattern. Repeat until 10 rows have been worked. Fasten off yarn.

speckle

see base design on page 60

variation 2

Double slant Work as given for main pattern using yarns E, D and A, working as main block with the following changes: **Row 9:** work 1st FPdtr into 1st dc on Row 4, then into every FPdtr as before, ending with 3dc. **Row 12:** as per Variation 1, making sure the 1st FPdtr gets worked into the 2nd FPdtr of Row 9. **Row 15:** work 1st FPdtr into 1st st on Row 10, then into every FPdtr as before, ending with 3dc.

variation 4

Double colours Work as given for main pattern using yarns B and C, working as main block with all FPdtr rows in 1 colour.

variation 3

Double speckles Work as given for main pattern using yarns C, B and E. Work as main block until 1st FPdtr, * work 2 FPdtr, 2dc, rep from * to last st, 1dc in last st. Repeat this on all FPdtr rows.

variation 5

Alternating speckles Work as given for main pattern using yarns E, B and A, working as main block with the following changes: **Row 9:** ch1, 1dc into next 4 sts, * FPdtr in next st as before, 1dc into each of next 2sts, rep from * ending with 1dc in each of last st. **Row 15:** work as Row 9.

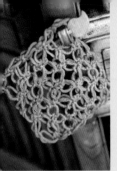

soloman's knot

see base design on page 63

variation 2
Big Solomon Using yarn C, work as given
for main pattern, but keep loops 5cm
(2 inches) long.

variation 4
Mohair Using yarn C, work as given for
main pattern.

variation 3
Hoopla yarn Using a 12mm hook and yarn F,
work as given for main pattern, but with
hoopla yarn.

variation 5
Sparkle Using yarn E, work as given for
main pattern.

variations

the wall

see base design on page 64

variation 2
Brick wall Work as given for main pattern, working Row 1 in yarn A and Row 2 in yarn B for wall effect, with changing colours every row.

variation 3
Paving stitch Using yarn C, ch15+4 for turning. **Row 1:** 1tr into 5th ch from hook, 1tr into next 3ch, * ch1, sk1, 1tr into next 4sts, rep from * once more, ch1, sk1, 1tr into last st, turn. **Row 2:** ch2, 1dc into first ch sp, *ch4, 1dc into next ch sp, rep from * once more, ch4, 1dc into tch sp, turn. **Row 3:** ch4, work * 4tr into 4-ch loop. ch1, sk1, rep from * twice more, ending 1tr into tch, turn. Rows 2–3 form the pattern; repeat to required length.

variation 4
Clustered paving stitch Using yarn D, ch15+3 for turning. **Row 1:** work 1 3tr cl into 4th ch from hook, * ch1, sk1, 3tr cl into next, rep from * 5 more times, ch1, 1tr into last ch, turn. **Row 2:** ch2, 1tr into 1st ch sp, * ch2, 1dc into next ch sp. Repeat from * 5 more times, ch2, 1tr into tch sp, turn. **Row 3:** ch4, work as Row 1, working the 3tr cl into the 2ch sp. Repeat pattern to required length using the picture as a guide.

variation 5
Granite stitch Using yarn E, ch15+2 for turning. **Row 1:** 1dc into 3rd ch from hook, * ch1, sk1, 1dc into next ch, rep from * to end, turn. **Row 2:** ch2, work 1dc into 1st ch sp, * ch1, 1dc into next ch sp, rep from * to end, turn. Row 2 forms the pattern; repeat to required length.

starry-eyed

see base design on page 67

variation 2
Beading Using yarn B, work as given for main pattern, threading beads onto the yarn before starting and adding beads as desired.

variation 4
Double treble crochet Using yarn C, ch26. **Row1:** 1dtr into the 10th ch from hook, work as given for main pattern, working in dtr throughout with ch4 for turning.

variation 3
Half treble crochet Using yarn B, ch25. **Row 1:** 1htr into the 9th st from hook, work as given for main pattern, working in htr throughout with ch2 for turning.

variation 5
Double crochet Using yarn D, ch23. **Row 1:** 1dc into 8th ch from hook, work as given for main pattern, working in dc throughout with ch1 for turning.

variations

harlequin

see base design on page 68

variation 2
Starburst stitch
Using yarn C,
ch24+1. **Row 1:** 9tr
into 5th ch from
hook, * sk3, 1dc into
next ch, sk3, 9tr into
next ch, rep from * sk3, 1dc into last ch, turn.
Row 2: ch3, sk 1st st, tr4tog over next 4sts, *
ch3, 1dc into next st, ch3, tr9tog over next
9sts, rep from * once more, ch3, tr5tog over
last 4sts plus tch, turn. **Row 3:** ch3, work 3tr
into top of tr5tog, * sk3ch, 1dc into next st,
sk3ch, 9tr into top of tr9tog, rep from * once
more, sk3ch,1dc into next st, sk3ch, 4tr into
top of tr4tog, turn. **Row 4:** ch3, *tr9tog over
next 9sts, ch3, 1dc into next st, ch3, rep from
* ending last rep with 1dc into top of tch.
Row 5: ch1, * sk3ch, 9tr into top of tr9tog,
sk3ch, 1dc into next st, rep from * to end,
turn. Rows 2–5 form the pattern. Repeat to
required length.

variation 3
**Two-colour
Starburst stitch**
Work as given for
Variation 2, using
yarn D for Row 1, yarn C for Rows 2–3 and
yarn D for Rows 4–5.

variation 4
Disc stitch Using
yarn E, ch16
(multiples of 8). **Row
1:** work 6tr into 4th
ch from hook, sk3, ss
into next ch, * sk
ch3, 6tr into next, sk3, ss into next ch, rep
from * to end, turn so the underside of ch is
facing. **Row 2:** sk3, 6tr
into next ch, sk3, ss into next, rep from * to
end. Make as many strips as desired, and
using the same yarn and a darning needle,
stitch the rows of discs together to make
a textured weave.

variation 5
Multicolour disc stitch As per Variation 4,
working each motif in a different colour.

variations

crocodile

see base design on page 71

variation 2

Feathers Work as given for main pattern, working each 'scale' as a feather instead, replacing the 5tr on 1st post with 1htr, 2tr, 2dtr and the 5trs on the 2nd post with 2dtr, 2tr, 1htr.

variation 4

Leaves Using yarn D, work as given for main pattern, adding a 3ch picot to the tip of each scale.

variation 3

Parrot feathers Work as given for Variation 2, working Rows 1–2 in yarn E, Rows 3–4 in yarn G, Rows 5–6 in yarn E, Rows 7–8 in yarn C and Rows 9–10 in yarn E.

variation 5

Autumn leaves Work as given for Variation 4, working Rows 1–2 in yarn D, Rows 3–4 in yarn B, Rows 5–6 in yarn D, Rows 7–8 in yarn A and Rows 9–10 in yarn D.

variations

bullion

see base design on page 72

variation 2

Bullion in a different colour Work as given for main pattern, working every bullion st in yarn B.

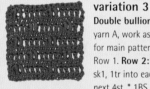

variation 3

Double bullion Using yarn A, work as given for main pattern for Row 1. **Row 2:** ch3, sk1, 1tr into each of next 4st, * 1BS in next 2st, 1tr into each of next 5st, rep from * ending last rep after 2tr. **Row 3:** work as Row 3 in main pattern. **Row 4:** ch3, sk1, 1tr into next st, * 1BS in each of next 2st, 1tr into each of next 5st, rep from * to end, working last tr into top of tch, turn. **Row 5:** work as Row 3. **Row 6:** work as Row 2. **Row 7:** work as Row 3. **Row 8:** work as Row 4. **Row 9:** work as Row 3. **Row 10:** work as Row 2. **Row 11:** work as Row 3. Fasten off.

variation 4

Vertical bullion lines Using yarn B, work as follows:
Row 1: work as Row 1 in main pattern.
Row 2: ch3, sk1, 1tr into next st, * 1BS into next st, 1tr into next 2sts, repeat from* 3 more times, 1BS into next st, 1tr into last st, turn. **Row 3:** work as Row 3 in main pattern. Rows 2–3 form the pattern. Repeat until 11 rows have been worked. Fasten off.

variation 5

Full-on bullion Using yarn B, work as follows: **Row 1:** work as Row 1 in main pattern. **Row 2:** ch3, sk1, work 1BS into every st to end, 1BS into top of tch, turn. **Row 3:** ch1, sk1, 1dc into each st to end, 1dc into top of tch turn. Rows 2–3 form the pattern. Repeat until 9 rows have been worked. Fasten off.

curlicues

see base design on page 75

variation 2
Little curlicues Using yarn C, work as given
for main pattern, working each curlicue as
follows: ch6, 2dc in 2nd ch from hook, 3dc in
each of next ch4.

variation 4
Little curlicues en masse Using yarn B,
work as given for main pattern, working
each curlicue as per Variation 2 in every
other stitch.

variation 3
Increased curlicues Using yarn D, work as
given for main pattern, working each curlicue
as follows: ch6, 3dc in 2nd ch from hook,
3htr in next st, 3tr in next st, 3dtr in next st,
3trtr in last st.

variation 5
Giant curlicues Using yarn E, work as given
for main pattern with following changes for
Rows 3 and 5. **Row 3:** ch3, 1tr into each of
next 4sts, * ch10, 3dtr in 4th ch from hook,
3dtr in each of next 6ch, ss in top of last tr
worked in main fabric, 1tr in each of next
5sts, rep from * to end, turn. **Row 5:** work as
main pattern, working curlicues as Row 3.

variations

trellis

see base design on page 76

variation 2
Double treble crochet Using yarn B, ch25. **Row 1:** 1dtr in the 5th ch from the hook, * ch1, 1dtr, rep from * to end, turn. **Row 2:** ch4, sk1 * 1dtr into ch1, 1ch, rep from * to end, working last dtr into top of tch, turn. Row 2 forms the pattern; repeat to required length.

variation 3
Stitch mix Using yarn C, ch24. Work Row 1 as given for main pattern. Fasten off yarn C and join in yarn B. **Row 2:** ch4, sk1 * 1dtr into ch1, ch1, rep from * to end, working last dtr into top of tch. Fasten off yarn B and join in yarn C. **Row 3:** ch3, 1tr into 1st st, * 1ch, 1tr in next ch, rep from * to end, turn. Rows 2–3 form the pattern; repeat 3 more times, keeping stripe sequence as set.

variation 4
Lattice shell Using yarn C, ch25. **Row 1:** 1dc in 2nd ch from hook and every ch to end, turn. **Row 2:** ch3, sk2, work * (3tr, ch2, 3tr) into next st, sk2, 1tr into next st, sk2 rep from * to last st, 1tr into last st. Row 2 forms the pattern; repeat to required length.

variation 5
Double lattice stitch Using yarn A, ch28. **Row 1:** 1dc into 2nd st from hook, 1dc into each st to end, turn. **Row 2:** ch1, 1dc into 1st 3sts, * ch5, sk3, 1dc into next 3sts, rep from * to end, turn. **Row 3:** ch1, 1dc into 1st 2sts, * ch3, 1dc into ch5sp, ch3, sk1 **, 1dc into next st, sk1, rep from * ending last rep at **, 1dc in each of last 2st, turn. **Row 4:** ch3, 1tr into 1st st, ch2, * 1dc into each of the next (ch3sp, 1dc ch3 sp) **, ch5, rep from * 3 more times, ending last rep at **, ch2, sk1,1tr into the last st and tch, turn. **Row 5:** ch1, dc into 1st 2sts, * ch3, sk next ch2 and 1dc, 1dc into next st, ch3 **, 1dc in ch5sp, rep from *, ending last rep at **, 1dc into last st and tch, turn. **Row 6:** ch1, 1dc into 1st 2sts, 1dc into next ch3sp, * ch5, work 1dc in next to the next (ch3sp, dc, ch3sp), rep from * twice more, ch1dc into last ch3sp, 1dc into last 2sts, turn. Rows 3–6 form the pattern. Repeat once more. **Next row:** ch1, 1dc into 1st 2sts, * 3dc in ch5sp, 1dc into next 3sts, rep from * to end, turn. **Next row:** ch1, 1dc into each st to end. Fasten off.

daisy chain

see base design on page 79

variation 2

Blossom stitch Row 1: ch5, 2tr cl into 4th ch from hook. * ch4, 2tr cl into 4th ch from hook, rep from * 3 times. Turn. **Row 2:** ch7, petal (2tr cl) in 4th ch from hook, * 1dc between petals of Row 1, ch4, make petal. Repeat from *, end 1tr in first ch of Row 1. Turn. **Row 3:** ch7, petal in 4th ch from hook, * ch4, make petal, skip 2 petals, 1dc in dc, ch4, make petal, rep from *, end ch4, make petal, 1tr in ch-sp. Turn. **Row 4:** ch7, Petal in 4th ch from hook, * ch4, make petal, skip 2 petals, 1 dc in between next 2 petals of previous row, ch4, make petal, rep from *, end 1 tr in ch-sp. Turn. Repeat Row 4.

variation 3

Blossom sdtripes Work Rows 1–4 as for Variation 2. **Row 5:** ch1, 1dc into first st. * Ch3, ss to top of petal. Repeat from * along, 1dc into last st. Turn. **Row 6:** ch1, * work 3dc into ch sp, 1 dc into dc. Repeat from * along. Turn. **Row 7:** ch3, sk1, 1tr into each st to end. **Row 8:** * ch4, 2dtr cl into 4th ch from hook, sk3, 1dc into next. Repeat from * to end. Turn. **Rows 9–12:** as Rows 2–4.

variation 4

Delta stitch Ch20. **Row 1:** ch4, 1dtr in 9th ch from hook. * Sk4, 1dtr into next, ch4, 1dtr into same st. rep from * to end. Turn. **Row 2:** ch4, 1dtr into top of 2dtr 'triangle' on row below. Repeat from * to end. Turn. **Row 3:** ch4, sk ch, 1dtr into top of next 2dtr 'triangle'. Ch4, 1dtr into same. Repeat from * to end. Turn.

variation 5

Filet daisies Ch21. **Row 1:** 1tr into 5th ch from hook. * Ch1, sk1, 1tr into next, 1 puff st into next, 1tr into next, ch1, sk1, 1tr into next, ch1, sk1, 1tr into next. Repeat from * to end. Turn. **Row 2:** ch4 (counts as 1tr, ch1), sk ch sp, 1tr into top of tr. * 1 puff stitch into ch sp, 1tr into next st, ch1, sk 1, 1tr into next, 1 puff stitch into ch sp, 1tr into next st, ch1, sk1, 1tr into next, 1 puff stitch into ch sp, 1tr into next, ch1, sk1, 1tr into next st, 1 puff stitch into ch sp, 1tr into next, ch1, sk1, 1tr into last. Turn. **Row 3:** ch4, sk ch sp, 1tr into next st. Work as Row 1. Turn. **Row 4:** ch4, sk ch sp, 1tr into next st, * ch1, sk1, 1tr into next st, rep from * to end, turn. Repeat Rows 1–4, working ch5, sk1, 1tr into next at start of row (counts as 1tr, ch2).

peacock

see base design on page 80

variation 2

Coloured peacock feathers Work as per main pattern using the following colours: Row 1 in yarn B, Row 2 in yarn A, Row 3 in yarn C, Row 4 in yarn A, Row 5 in yarn D, Row 6 in yarn A, Row 7 in yarn E and Row 8 in yarn A to complete the pattern.

variation 3

Framed peacock tails Using yarn A, ch15+1. **Row 1:** work as given for Row 1 of Variation 1. Fasten off yarn A and join in yarn E. **Row 2:** ch4, 1dtr into dc, 1Etr into next st, 1tr into next st, 1htr into next st, 1dc into each of the next 6sts, 1htr into next st, 1tr into next, 1Etr into next, 1dtr into each of the next 2 sts, turn. **Row 3:** ch3, 1tr into each st to end, turn. Rows 1–3 form the pattern. Repeat to required length.

variation 4

Turtle stitch Using yarn D, work a multiple of 6ch+4, (add 3ch for turning). **Row 1:** 3tr into 4th ch from hook, sk2, 1dc into next ch, * sk2, 5tr into next ch, sk2, 1dc into next ch, rep from * to end, turn. **Row 2:** ch3, 3tr into back loop of st, * sk2, 1dc into next st (centre of 5tr), sk2, 5tr into next st, rep from *ending last rep with ss into top of tch, turn. Row 2 forms the pattern; repeat to required length.

variation 5

Sweet pea stitch Multiple of 6ch+4 (add 3 for turning) Using yarn F, ch25. **Row 1:** 1tr into 4th ch from hook, * sk2, 5tr into next ch, sk1, 1tr into each of the next 2ch, rep from * to last 3 sts, sk2, 3tr into last, turn. **Row 2:** ch3, 1tr in between first 2sts, * 5tr between next 2tr, 1tr between 2nd and 3rd of 5tr, 1tr between 3rd and 4th of 5tr, rep from * to end, working 3tr in between the last 2tr, turn. Row 2 forms the pattern; repeat to required length.

variations

fruit punch

see base design on page 83

variation 2
Raised pineapples
Using yarn C, ch20.
Row 1: 1dc into
2nd ch from hook,
1dc into each ch to
end, turn. **Rows
2–3:** ch1, 1dc into each st to end, turn. **Row
4:** ch1, 1dc into 1st 3sts, join in yarn A,
* work 1 pineapple into same stitch 2 rows
below (1RP=raised pineapple worked). With
yarn C, work 1dc into next 3 sts, rep from * to
end, turn. **Rows 5–7:** work as Row 2. Row 8:
ch1, 1dc into first st, * 1RP into next st, 1dc
into next 3sts, rep from * 3 more times, 1RP
into next st, 1dc into last st, turn. Rows 2–8
form the pattern. Repeat once more, then
Rows 2–3. Fasten off.

variation 3
Strawberries Work as
per Variation 4, working
Row 4 in yarn E.

variation 4
Blackberries Ch18.
With yarn C, work 3
blackberries. Using
yarn C, work Rows
1–3 as given for
Variation 2. Work
Row 4 as given for Variation 2, using yarn D
for RP to make blackberries. Work Row 5 as
Row 2 using yarn B.

variation 5
Spiky pineapples
Work as per
Variation 2, with
the addition of
leaves. Make a
pineapple and let
yarn A fall behind. Pull through yarn B. Make
3 picots – ch3, 1ss into 3rd ch from hook. Ss
picot leaves to RP. Let yarn B fall behind.
Continue with pattern, working 7 rows of dc
between pineapple rows. Using yarn C, work
Rows 1–3 as per main pattern. **Row 4:** ch1,
1dc into 1st 3sts, join in yarn A, * work 1
pineapple into same stitch 2 rows below
(1RP, raised pineapple worked), join in yarn B
and work 3 picots as follows: (ch3, ss into 3rd
ch from hook) 3 times, ss picots to RP, with
yarn C work 1dc into next 3sts, rep from * to
end, turn.

variations

stand out

see base design on page 84

variation 2
Star Using yarn C, ch45. **Row 1:** 1tr into 5th ch from hook (counts as 1 tr and ch1), * ch1, sk1, 1tr into next, rep from * to end, turn. **Rows 2–17:** work from chart.

variation 4
Reverse cross Using yarn E, cc 20. **Row 1:** 1tr into 5th ch from hook. **Rows 2–7:** work from chart.

variation 3
Cross Using yarn D, ch20. **Row 1:** 1tr into 4th ch from hook. **Rows 2–7:** work from chart.

variation 5
Daisies Using yarn F, ch16. **Row 1:** 1tr into 5th ch from hook. **Rows 2–8:** work from chart.

broomstick lace

see base design on page 87

variation 2

Broomstick loops Using yarn D, ch20. **Row 1:** 1dc into 2nd ch from hook, 1dc into each ch to end. Do not turn work. **Row 2:** lengthen last loop and slip it onto needle. Hold needle in left hand, insert the hook into the next st, YOH, draw through the loop and place on needle, rep to end, do not turn. **Row 3:** slip 1st loop onto hook, YOH, and pull through 1st loop, insert hook under separate thread leading to new loop, YOH, pull through 2 loops, tr in each loop, slipping loop from needle. Rows 2–3 form the pattern. Work 4 rows in total. Fasten off.

variation 3

Colour stripe Work as given for main pattern, changing colour every 2 rows.

variation 4

Sweeping broomsticks Using yarn C, ch19. **Row 1:** 1dc into 2nd ch from hook, dc to end. Do not turn work. **Row 2:** as Row 2 of Variation 2. **Row 3:** * slip 6sts off needles and onto the hook from right to left, YOH, draw a loop through the 6 loops, work 6dc through the 6 loops, rep from * twice more, turn. **Row 4:** ch1, tr to end. Do not turn work. Repeat Rows 2–5.

variation 5

Yarn variation Work as given for main pattern, or any of the variations, using yarn D.

tunisian crochet

see base design on page 88

variation 2
Tunisian purl stitch (TPS) Using yarn C, ch15. **Row 1:** work forwards and return as per main pattern.
Row 2 (forwards): * bring the yarn forward to the front of the work. Insert the hook under the single vertical thread, the same as the Tunisian simple stitch, then take the yarn to the back of the work, wrap it around the hook and pull through, keeping the loop on the hook, rep from * to end. **Row 2 (return):** as Row 1.

variation 3
Honeycomb Using yarn D, ch15. **Row 1:** work forwards and return as per main pattern. **Row 2 (forwards):** * 1TSS into 1st st, 1TPS into next st, rep from * to end, working a TSS into the last st. **Row 2 (return):** work as Row 1. **Row 3 (forwards):** * 1TPS into 1st st, 1TSS into 2nd st, rep from * to end working a TSS into the last st. **Row 3 (return):** work as Row 1. Rows 2–3 form the pattern; repeat to required length.

variation 4
Crossed stitch Using yarn B, ch15. Work Row 1 forwards and return as per main pattern. **Row 2 (forwards):** sk2, insert hook into the 3rd vertical bar, YOH, pull loop through (2 loops on hook), insert the hook into the next 2 vertical from right to left, YOH, pull loop through, * sk1, insert hook into next st, YOH, pull loop through, insert hook into skipped vertical bar, YOH, pull loop through, rep from * to end. Do not turn. **Row 2 (return):** work as Row 1. Row 2 forms the pattern.; repeat to required length.

variation 5
Bias stitch Using yarn E, ch15. Work Row 1 forwards and return as per main pattern. **Row 2 (forwards):** sk1, * keeping all loops on hook, skip next vertical bar, insert hook from right to left under next vertical bar, YOH, and draw up a loop, insert hook from right to left under skipped vertical bar, YOH, and draw up a loop. Repeat from * across. Do not turn. **Row 2 (return):** work as per main pattern. Row 2 forms the pattern; repeat to required length.

more tunisian crochet

variation 2

Tunisian chain lace Using yarn C, ch16. **Row 1 (forwards):** * sk ch1, insert hook in next ch and pull loop through, ch1, rep from * to end, keeping all loops on hook. **Row 1 (return):** YOH and pull loop through* ch1, YOH and pull through 2 loops, rep from * until 1 loop remains on hook. **Row 2 (forwards):** ch1 * sk next ch sp, insert hook in next as in TKS. Yarn over and pull up a loop, chain 1. Repeat from * across, keeping all loops on hook. **Row 2 (return):** work as Row1, return row. Row 2 forms the pattern; repeat to required length.

variation 3

Filet Using D, ch17. **Row 1 (forwards):** sk5ch, * YOH 3 times (twice for skipped stitches, once for the Tdc), insert hook in next ch, YOH, pull loop through, YOH, and pull through 2 loops, skch2, rep from * to end, keeping all loops and yo's on hook. **Row1 (return):** as Row 1 return of main pattern. **Row 2 (forwards):** ch2 * sk2, YOH 3 times (twice for skipped stitches, once for the Tdc), insert hook in next ch, YOH, pull loop through, YOH, and pull through 2 loops, skch2, rep from * to end, keeping all loops and yos on hook. **Row 2 (return):** work as Row 1 return. Row 2 forms the pattern; repeat to required length.

see base design on page 91

variation 4

Double Tunisian crochet st Using yarn C,
ch16. **Row 1 (forwards):** YOH, insert into 3rd
ch from hook, YOH, pull through loop, YOH,
pull through 2 loops, (keep 1 loop on hook) *
YOH and insert hook into next ch, YOH, and
pull loop through, YOH, and pull through 2
loops, rep from * keeping all loops on hook.
Row 1 (return): as Row 1 return of main
pattern, ch2. **Row 2 (forwards):** * YOH and
insert hook under next vertical bar, YOH,
pull loop through, YOH, pull through 2 loops,
rep from * keeping all loops on hook. **Row 2
(return):** work as Row 1, ch2. Row 2 forms
the pattern; repeat to required length.

variation 5

Cluster Using A, ch17. **Row 1 (forwards):** as
Row 1 forwards. **Row 1 (return):** YOH, pull
back through 3 loops, * ch3, YOH and pull
through 5 loops, rep from * to last 3ch, ch3
and pull through last 4 loops. **Row 2
(forwards):** sk1 1st cluster, * yoh, pull loop
through from each of the ch3 in the next ch
sp, pull up a loop from the closing ch of the
cluster in prev row, rep from * to end. **Row 2
(return):** YOH and pull back through 3 loops.
* ch3, yoh and draw through 5 loops, rep
from * to last 4 loops, ch3 and pull through
last 4 loops. Row 2 forms the pattern; repeat
to required length.

round and round

Now that you've mastered the basic techniques of crochet, it's time to get creative with them. In this chapter you'll learn how to crochet in the round and discover all sorts of new patterns and configurations, starting with an old favorite: the classic granny square.

classic granny square

Main pattern: using yarn A, ch6, join with ss to make a ring.

Round 1: ch3 (counts as 1tr) 2tr into ring, ch2, * 3tr into ring, ch2, rep from * twice more, join with ss into top of ch3, turn.

Round 2: ch3 (counts as 1tr), 2tr, 2ch, 3tr into 1st ch2sp, * ch1, 3tr, 2ch, 3tr into next ch2sp, rep from * twice more, ch1, join with ss into top of ch3, turn.

Round 3: ch3 (counts as 1tr), 2tr, into 1st ch sp, ch1,* 3tr, ch2, 3tr into next ch2sp (first corner), ch1, 3tr into next ch sp, ch1 rep from * twice more, 3tr, 2ch, 3tr into last ch2sp, ch1, join with ss into top of ch3, turn.

Round 4: ch3 (counts as 1tr), 2tr into 1st ch sp, ch1, * 3tr, ch2, 3tr into next ch2sp, (ch1, 3tr into next ch sp) twice, ch1, rep from * twice more, 3tr, ch2, 3tr, into next ch2sp, ch1, 3tr into last ch sp, ch1, join with ss into top of ch3. Fasten off.

materials

- ▨ 4mm hook
- ▨ Sublime Baby Cashmere Merino Silk DK in Purple (A), Green (B), Raspberry (C)

see other variations on page 150

variation 1

Flowering Work as given for main pattern using yarn A for Rounds 1, 3 and 5, and yarn B for Rounds 2 and 4.

solid granny square

Main pattern: using yarn A, ch5, join with ss to form a ring.

Round 1: ch3 (counts as 1tr), 2tr into ring, * ch3 (1st corner worked), 3tr into ring, rep from * twice more, ch3, join with ss into top of ch3 at beg of round.

Round 2: ch3 (counts as 1tr), * 1tr each st, (3tr, ch3, 3tr) into corner sp, rep from * to last st, 1tr into top of ch 3 of prev round, join with ss into top of ch3 at beg of round.

Round 3-5: work as for Row 2. Fasten off.

materials

- 4mm hook
- King Cole Bamboo Cotton DK in 526 Moss (A), 523 Yellow (B), 576 Aqua (C), 529 Plum (D), 543 Oyster (E)

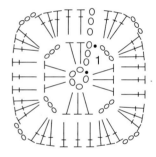

variation 1

see other variations on page 151

Colour changing rounds Work as given for main pattern. Rounds 1, 3 and 5, work in yarn A. For Rounds 2 and 4, work in yarn B.

patchwork

Main pattern: using yarn A, ch6, join with ss to form a ring.

Round 1: 3ch (counts as 1tr), 2tr into ring, 2ch, * 3tr into ring, 2ch. Rep from * twice more, join with ss into ch3, turn. Break off yarn A and join in yarn B.

Round 2: ch3 (counts as 1tr), 2tr, ch2, 3tr into 1st ch2sp (1st corner worked), ch1, * 3tr, ch2, 3tr into next ch2sp, ch1, rep from * to end, join with ss into ch3, turn. Break off yarn B and join in yarn C.

Round 3: ch3 (counts as 1tr), 2tr into 1st ch2sp, ch1, * 3tr, ch2, 3tr into 1st ch2sp, ch1 **, 3tr into next ch1sp, ch1, rep from * ending last rep at **, join with ss into ch3. Fasten off yarn.

Join squares together using yarn C. With wrong sides together, work a dc into each of the sts on the straight edges and work 3dc into the corners.

materials

- 4mm hook
- King Cole Smooth Double Knit in Raspberry (A), Green (B), Blue (C), Grey (D)

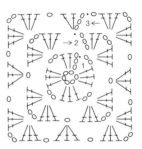

....

see other variations on page 152

variation 1

Colour frame Using yarn C, ch6, join with ss to form a ring. **Round 1:** as given for main pattern. Do not break off yarn C, join in yarn D. **Round 2:** ch1, * 1dc, ch2, 1dc into 1st corner, ch3, rep from * 3 more times, join with ss into ch1, join in yarn C back in. **Round 3:** ch3 (counts as 1tr) 2tr, ch3, 3tr into ch2sp, * ch1, 3tr, ch3, 3tr into next ch2sp, rep from * to end, join with ss into ch3. Make a further 3 squares, working 1 more in yarn C and D, then a further 2 in yarn B and D. Using the picture as a guide, join the squares together using yarn D and dc. Work edge using yarn D as follows: ss into1 st sp, sk1 * 3tr into the sp, sk1, rep from * all working 3tr, 2ch, 3tr into the corner spaces.

wagon wheels

Main pattern: using yarn A, ch4, join with ss to form a ring.

Round 1: ch1 (counts as 1dc), 11dc into ring, join with ss into tch.

Round 2: ch6 (counts as 1dtr and 2ch), 1dtr into next st, * ch2, 1dtr into next st, rep from * to end, ch2, join with ss into 4th ch at beg of round.

Round 3: ch5 (counts as 1dtr and ch1), * 1dtr into ch2sp, ch1, 1dtr into next st, ch1, rep from * to end, join with ss into 4th ch at beg of round. Fasten off A and join in B.

Round 4: ch3 (counts as 1tr), 2tr, ch3, 3tr into 1st ch1sp (1st corner worked), ch1, * (1tr, ch1) into each of the next 5 ch1sp **, (3tr, ch3, 3tr) into next ch1sp, ch1, rep from * ending last rep at **, join with ss into top of tch.

Round 5: ss into 1st 2sts and 1st ch3sp, ch3 (counts as 1tr), 2tr, ch3, 3tr into same ch3sp (1st corner worked), * ch1, 3tr into next ch1sp, sk next ch1sp, ch1, (3tr into next ch1sp, ch1) twice, sk next ch sp, 3tr into next ch1sp, ch1 **, work (3tr, ch3, 3tr) into next ch3sp, rep from * ending last rep at **, join with ss into top of ch3. Ss into next 2sts and ch3sp. Fasten off B and join in C.

Round 6: ch3 (counts as 1tr) 2tr into 1sts ch3sp, ch3, 2tr into same sp, (1st corner worked), * 3 tr into each of the next 4 ch1sp's **, (3tr, ch3, 3tr) into next ch3sp, rep from * ending last rep at **, join with ss into top of ch3.

materials

- 4mm hook
- Sublime Baby Cashmere Merino Silk DK in Caterpillar (A), Ragdoll (B), Teddy Red (C)

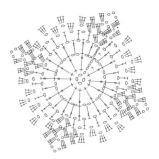

see other variations on page 153

variation 1

Solid edge Work Rounds 1–3 as given for main pattern. For Rounds 4–5, work as given for main pattern, working 1tr into the top of each st, instead of working * sk3, 3tr.

meadow square

Main pattern: using yarn A, ch6, join with ss to form a ring.

Round 1: ch1 (counts as 1tr), 11dc into ring, join with ss into tch.

Round 2: ch1, 3tr into 1st st, * ch1, ss into next st, ch1, 3tr into next st, rep from * 5 more times to make 6 petals, join with ss into back loop of ch1. Work next round at the back of the work to create 4 loops.

Round 3: * ch3, miss 1st petal, ss into centre st of next, rep from * to end, join with ss into 1st ch at beg of round. Break off yarn A and join in yarn D.

Round 4: ch3 (counts as 1tr), 2tr, ch3, 3tr into 1st ch3 loop, ch1, work (3tr, ch3, 3tr) into next ch3 loop, ch1, rep from * to end, join with ss into tch.

Next round: work pattern as given for granny square, with 3trs into each ch1sp, and (3tr, ch3, 3tr) into corner of ch3 sp. Repeat the last round to required size.

Project notes: Baby blanket. Use a 5.5mm hook, Rowan Kid Classic in Tea Rose, Lavender Ice, Tattoo, and Teal. Using a 5.5mm hook and Rowan Kid Classic yarn, ch4, join with ss.

Make up 20 squares, 5 of each colour centre, and join together. Add a shell edging for a beautiful gift: sk2, 5tr into next st, sk2, ss into next. Repeat shells around for edging.

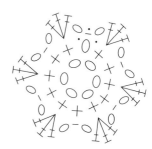

see other variations on page 154

variation 1

Daisy centre square Using yarn E, ch6, join with ss to form a ring. **Round 1:** work as given for main pattern. Break off yarn E and join in yarn F. **Round 2:** ch4, 1dtr into 1st st, ch4, ss into next st, * ch4, 1dtr into next st, ch4, ss into next st, rep from * ending last rep with ss into back loop of base of ch4 at beg of round. Break off yarn F and join in yarn D. **Rounds 3–5:** work as given for main pattern. Fasten off.

posy square

Main pattern: using yarn A, ch4, join with ss to form a ring.

Round 1: ch3 (counts as 1tr), 11tr into ring, join with ss into tch.

Round 2: * ch1, 3tr into next st, ch1, ss into next st, rep from * 5 more times, join with ss to back loop of ch. Break of yarn A, join in yarn B. Work next round at the back of the work.

Round 3: ch3, sk 1st petal, 1dc into back of tr below next dc in round 1, * ch3, sk next petal, 1dc into tr below next dc in Round 1, rep from * ss into base of ch3 at beg of round.

Round 4: ss into 1st ch3sp, work (1dc, 5tr, 1dc) into 1st and every

foll ch3 sp to end, join with ss into base of 1dc at beg of round.

Round 5: ss into back of 1dc of 1st petal, ch3, * sk next 9sts, ss into back of next st, ch3, rep from * ending last rep with ss into base of ch3. Break off yarn B and join in yarn C.

Round 6: ch3 (counts as 1tr), 2tr into 1st ch3 loop, ch2, 3tr into same loop, ch1, * work (3tr, ch2, 3tr) into next ch3 loop, ch1, rep from * to end, join with ss into top of ch3.

Round 7: work pattern as given for granny square, with 3trs into each ch1 sp, and (3tr, ch3, 3tr) into corner ch3sp. Repeat last round to required size. Fasten off.

materials

- 4mm hook
- Debbie Bliss Rialto DK in Duck Egg (A), White (B), Emerald (C), Apple (D), Gold (E), Scarlet (F)

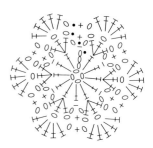

see other variations on page 155

variation 1

Two-tone flower Work as given for main pattern. Rounds 1–3 in yarn A, Round 4 in yarn C and Rounds 5–7 in yarn B.

claude

Main pattern: using yarn B, ch4, join with ss into a ring.

Round 1: ch1 (counts as 1dc), 11dc into ring, join with ss into ch1. Break off yarn B and join in yarn A.

Round 2: ch3, tr into same st, * sk2, ch7, 2tr into next st, rep from * 3 more times, ch7, join with ss to top of ch3.

Round 3: ch2, work (1dc, 1htr, 2tr, 2dtr, 1trtr, 2dtr, 2tr, 1htr, 1dc) into 1st 7ch loop (1st petal worked), * ch2, 1tr in between next 2tr, ch2, work (1dc, 1htr, 2tr, 2dtr, 1trtr, 2dtr, 2tr, 1htr, 1dc) into next 7ch loop, rep from * twice more, ch2, join with ss into base of ch2. Break off yarn B and join in yarn C. Work next round at back of work.

Round 4: ch9 (counts as 1dtr and ch5), sk ch2 and next 4sts, ss into back of next st, * ch5, sk next 4sts and ch2, 1dtr into next st, ch5, sk ch2 and next 4sts, ss into back of next st, rep from * twice more, ch5, sk next 4sts and ch2, join with ss into 4th of ch5.

Round 5: ss into 1st ch5sp, ch3 (counts as 1tr), 2tr into same sp, ch1,* (3tr, ch3, 3tr) into next ch5sp (1st corner worked), ch1, 3tr into next ch5sp, ch1, rep from * twice more, 3tr, ch3, 3tr into last ch5sp, ch1, join with ss into top of ch3.

Round 6 onwards: work pattern as given for granny square, with 3tr's into each ch1sp, and (3tr, ch3, 3tr) into corner ch3sp. Repeat last round to required size. Fasten off.

materials

- 4mm hook
- Sublime Baby Cashmere Merino Silk DK in Vanilla (A), Cheeky (B), Caterpillar (C), Gooseberry (D), Ragdoll (E), Little Miss Plum (F), Teddy Red (G), Seesaw (H),

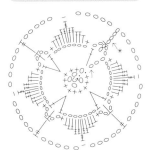

see other variations on page 156

variation 4

Aster Using yarn I, ch4, join with ss into a ring. **Round 1:** ch1 (counts as 1dc), 7dc into ring, join with ss into ch1. Fasten off yarn I and join in yarn D. **Round 2:** * ch7, ss into 2nd ch from hook to make picot, 1dc into each of the remaining ch4, ss into next st, rep from * to ending last rep with ss into base of ch7. Fasten off yarn D and join in yarn F to tip of 1st petal. **Round 3:** * ch6, ss into tip of next petal, rep from * to end. **Round 4:** work as given for Round 4 of Variation 3, working into each ch6sp. **Round 5:** work as given for Round 6 of main pattern.

claude 137

let it snow

Main pattern: With yarn A, ch6, join with ss to form a ring.

Round 1: ch3, 15tr in ring, join with ss into tch.

Round 2: ch5 (counts as 1tr and ch2), tr into base of ch, sk1, * (1tr, ch2, 1tr) next st, sk1, rep from * 6 times, join with ss into 3rd of ch5.

Round 3: ss into 1st ch sp, ch3 (counts as 1tr), work (1tr, ch3, 2tr) in same sp, * (2tr, ch3, 2tr) into next ch2sp, rep from * 6 more times, join with a ss into top of ch3.

Round 4: ss into next st and next ch3sp, ch3 (counts as 1tr), (2tr, ch3, 3tr) into same sp, work * (3tr, ch3, 3tr) into next ch3sp, rep from * 6 more times, join with a ss into top of ch3.

Round 5: ss in next 2sts and in next ch3sp, ch3, (3tr, ch2, 4tr), * (4tr, ch2, 4tr) into next ch3sp, rep from * 6 more times, join with ss into ch3. Break off yarn A and join in yarn B.

Round 6: ss into next 3sts and ch2sp, ch3 (counts as 1tr), 1tr, ch3, 2tr into same ch2sp, 1tr in between each of the next 5sts, 1htr in between next st, 1dc in between next st, ss into next ch2sp, dc in between next sts, 1htr in between next sts, 1tr in between next 5sts, * (2tr, ch3, 2tr) into next ch sp, 1tr in between next 5sts, 1htr in between next st, 1dc in between next st, ss into next ch2sp, 1dc in next sp, 1htr in between next st, 1tr in between next 5sts, rep from * twice more, join with ss into top of ch3.

Round 7: ch3, 1tr in next st, work (2tr, 3ch, 2tr) into next corner, * 1tr into next 7sts, 1htr, 1dc in next 2sts, 1htr, 1tr in next 7sts, work (2tr, 3ch, 2tr) into next corner, rep from * twice more, 1tr in next 7sts, 1htr, 1dc in next 2sts, 1htr, 1tr in last 5sts, join with ss into ch3. Fasten off.

materials

- 4mm hook: main, Var 2, 4, 5
- Sublime Baby Cashmere Merino DK in Vanilla (A), Teddy Red (B), Sailor Blue (C), Puffin (D), Skipper (E)
- 3mm hook: Var 1
- DMC Lumina (F)
- 12mm hook: Var 3
- hoopla yarn

variation 1
Wintertime Work as given for main pattern using yarn F.

see other variations on page 157

bullion in the round

Main pattern: using yarn A, ch6, join with ss to form a ring.

Round 1: ch3, 12BS into ring, join with ss into tch, hide ch3 behind first and last BS. Fasten off.

materials

- 6mm hook
- Sublime Chunky Merino Tweed in Glover (A), Roebuck (B), Forage (C)

see other variations on page 158

variation 1

Flat bullion Using yarn A, ch6, join with ss to form a ring. **Round 1:** ch3, 10tr into ring, join with ss into top of tch. Break off yarn A and join in yarn B. **Round 2:** ch3, 2BS into each tr to end, join with ss into top of tch. Fasten off.

spinning wheels

Main pattern: using yarn G, ch6, join with ss to form a ring.

Round 1: * ch5, 4dtr cl into ring, ch5, ss to ring (1st petal worked), rep from * 3 more times, join with ss into base of ch5.

Round 2: * ch2, 12dtr into top of cluster, ch2, ss into ss from prev round, rep from * ending last rep with ss into base of ch2.

Round 3: ss into ch2 and in between next 4sts, * ch5, 4BPdtr cl over next 4sts, ch5, ss in to sp in between 8th and 9th sts, ch5, work 8BPdtr cl into last 4sts of petal and 1st 4sts on next petal, ch5, ss into sp in between next st, rep from * 4 more times.

Round 4: * ch2, 12dtr into top of 1st cluster, ch2, ss into ss from prev round, ch2, 8dtr into top of next cluster, ch2, ss into ss from prev row, rep from * to end. Fasten off.

Project notes: Potholder. Using a 4.5mm hook and a colour-changing yarn (such as Araucania Chacacubo), and work the main pattern. Fasten off. Make a strap as follows: ch8, turn, work 1 tr into 4th ch from hook, and 1 tr into each st to end. Turn. * Ch3, sk1, 1tr into each st to end, turn. Rep from * until strap is of desired length. Fasten off, fold strap in half, and stitch to corner of block using a tapestry or darning needle.

materials

- 4mm hook
- Araucania Chacabuco (G)
- Sublime Baby Cashmere Merino Silk DK in Cheeky (A), Caterpillar (B), Piglet (C), Puzzle (D), Puffin (E), Ragdoll (F)

see other variations on page 159

variation 1

Two-colour block Work as given for main pattern working Rounds 1–2 in yarn B. Fasten off yarn, then join in yarn C in between 4th and 5th sts. Complete pattern as given for main work in yarn B. Fasten off.

climbing roses

Main pattern: using yarn A, ch4, join with ss to form a ring.

Round 1: ch1 (counts as 1dc), 11dc into ring, join with ss into ch1.

Round 2: ch1, 3tr into next st (1st petal worked), ch1, ss into next st, rep from * to end, ss into ch1. Work next round at the back of work to create 6 loops.

Round 3: ch3, sk petal, 1dc into back of ss, rep from * to end, join with ss into ch3. Fasten off yarn A and join in yarn B.

Round 4: ch1, 5tr into 1st ch3 loop, ch1, dc into next st, * 5tr into next ch3 loop, 1dc into next st, rep from * to end, join with ss into ch1. Work next round at the back of the work to create 4 loops.

Round 5: ss into back of 1st st, ch5, sk next petal and next 2 sts, * ss into next st (centre st of 5tr), ch5, sk5, rep from * ending last rep with ss into 1st ss, turn. Fasten off yarn B and join in yarn C.

Round 6: ss into 1st ch5 loop, ch3 (counts as 1 tr), 2tr, ch3, 3tr into same sp (1st corner worked), work

(3tr, ch3, 3tr) into next ch5 loop, join with ss to top of ch3.

Round 7: ch3 (counts as 1tr), 1tr into next 2sts, * work (2tr, ch3, 2tr) into next ch3sp (1st corner worked), 1tr into each st to next ch3sp, rep from * ending last rep once you have worked across the final sts, join with ss into ch3.

Round 8: ch4 (counts as 1tr and ch1), (sk1, 1tr into next st, ch1) twice, * work (2tr, ch3, 2tr) into ch3sp (1st corner worked), work (1tr into next st, ch1, sk1) twice,1tr into next 2sts, work (ch1, sk1, 1tr into next st) twice, ch1, 1tr into next st, rep from * ending last rep once you have worked across the final sts, join with ss to top of ch3.

materials

- 4mm hook
- Sublime Baby Cashmere Merino Silk DK in 04 Gooseberry (A), 246 Puffin (B), 245 Caterpillar (D), 244 Ragdoll (E), 192 Teddy Red (F), 03 Vanilla (G), 48 Cheeky (H), 195 Puzzle (I), 01 Piglet (J)
- Sublime Extra Fine Merino DK in 20 Mocha (C), 173 Passion (K)

Round 9: work as Round 8.

Round 10 onwards: work a solid row (like Round 7) to close off, or continue working a mesh pattern.

see other variations on page 160

doilies

Notes: MP=make picot

Main pattern: using yarn A, ch6, join with ss to form a ring.

Round 1: ch6 (counts as 1dtr and ch2), 1dtr into ring, * ch2, 1dtr into ring, rep from * 6 more times, join with ss to 4th ch of ch6.

Round 2: ss into first ch2sp, ch4, 4dtr into same ch2sp, ch2, * 5dtr into next ch2sp, ch2, rep from * to end, join with ss into top of tch.

Round 3: ch4, 1dtr into each of the next 4 sts, * (1dtr, ch3, 1dtr) into ch2sp **, 1dtr into next 5sts, rep from * ending last rep at **, join with ss to top of tch, turn.

Round 4: ch1, ss into 1st st, 1dc into next ch2sp, 6ch, sk1, dtr5tog over the next 5sts, ch6, 1dc into next ch2sp, rep from * to end, join with ss into dc at beg of row, turn.

Round 5: ch4, ss into 3rd ch from hook, MP, * 8dc into ch6sp, 1dc into top of dtr5tog, MP 3 more times, 1dc into top of dtr5tog, 8dc into next ch6sp, 1dc into next st, MP, rep from * to end, join with ss into base of 1st picot.

materials

- 4mm hook
- King Cole Bamboo Cotton DK in Yellow (A), Moss (B), Peacock (C), Oyster (D), Plum (E), Cobalt (F)

---

see other variations on page 161

variation 1

Mini star doily Using yarn D, ch4, join with ss to form a ring. **Round 1:** ch3 (counts as 1tr), 11tr into ring, join with ss into top of tch. **Round 2:** ch5 (counts as 1tr and ch2), 1tr into next st, ch2, 1tr into next st, ch2 rep from * to end, join with ss into top of tch. **Round 3:** ss into first ch2sp, work (1dc, 1hdtr, 3ch, 1hdtr, 1dc) into next and every foll ch2sp to end, join with ss into top of dc at beg of the round. **Round 4:** ss into next 2sts and into ch3sp, * ch5, 1dc into ch3sp, rep from * to end, join with ss into base of ch5. **Round 5:** work 3dc, 1 picot, 2dc into each ch sp around. Fasten off. **Round 6:** ch1, work (3dc, MP, 2dc) into next and every foll ch5sp to end, join with ss into tch. Fasten off. **Round 1:** 2tr cl into ring, ch2, * 3tr cl into ring, ch2, rep from * 6 more times, join with ss into ch3. **Round 2:** work as given for Round 2, Variation 2. **Round 3:** ch3 (counts as 1tr), 1tr, ch3, 2tr into ch2sp, 1dc into next ch2sp, * (2tr, ch3, 2tr) into next ch2sp, 1dc into next ch2sp, rep from * to end, join with ss into ch3.

maude

Main pattern: using yarn A, ch6, join with ss to form a ring.

Round 1: ch1, 11dc into ring, join with ss into ch1.

Round 2: ch4 (counts as 1tr and ch1), * 1tr into next st, ch1, rep from * to end, join with ss to 3rd of ch4.

Round 3: ch3 (counts as 1tr), 2tr into 1st ch sp, ch1, * 3tr into next ch sp, ch1, rep from * to end, join with ss into 3rd of ch4. Ss into each of the next 2tr and ch sp.

Round 4: ch5 (counts as 1tr and ch2), sk next st, * 1tr in between next 2sts, ch2, rep from * to end, join with ss into 3rd of ch5. Ss into each of the next ch2sp.

Round 5: ch1, 3dc into ch2sp,* 3dc into next ch2sp, rep from * to end, join with ss into ch1.

Round 6: ch3 (counts as 1tr), 2tr, ch2, 3tr into 1st st, ch1,* sk2, 3htr into next st, ch1, (sk2, 3dc into next st, ch1) 3 times, sk2, 3htr into next st, sk2, 3tr, ch2, 3tr into next st, rep from * to end, join with ss into top of ch3. Fasten off.

materials

- 12mm hook: main, Var 1–4
- King Cole Bamboo Cotton in Oyster (A), Rose (B), Aqua (C), Damson (D), Opal (E)
- 4mm hook: Var 5
- hoopla yarn

see other variations on page 162

variation 1

Lacy flower Using yarn D, work Rounds 1–2 as given for main pattern. **Round 3:** * ch6, ss into next ch sp, rep from * ending last rep with ss into base of ch6 at the beg of the round. Ss into 1st ch3 and this brings you up to the top of the arc. **Round 4:** ch3, 1tr into same sp, ch3, * 2tr into next ch6sp, ch3, rep from * to end, join with ss into top of ch3. Ss into next st and ch3 sp. **Round 5:** ss into 1st tr, * 4dc into ch3 sp, ss into next tr, rep from * to end, join with ss into 1st tr. **Round 6:** * (1tr into next st, tr into next st, tr into next st, dc into next st), rep from * to end, join with ss into top of tr at the beg of the round. Fasten off.

variations

classic granny square

see base design on page 125

variation 2

Middle flower Work as given for main pattern using yarn A for Rounds 1–3 and yarn B for Rounds 4–5.

variation 3

Bullseye Work as given for main pattern using hoopla jersey yarn.

variation 4

Double crochet and treble crochet Work as given for main pattern using yarn B for Round 1. **Round 2:** using yarn C, ch1 (counts as 1dc) 2dc into 1st ch2sp (first corner), * 1dc into next 3sts, 3dc into next ch2sp, rep from * twice more, 1dc into next 2sts and tch, turn. **Round 3:** using yarn A, ch3, 1tr into 1st 3sts, * 3tr into next st, 1tr into next 5sts, rep from * 3 more times, 3tr into next st. Repear Rows 2 and 3 for pattern using yarn C for Rounds 4 and 6, yarn B for Round 5 and yarn A for Round 7.

solid granny square

see base design on page 126

variation 2
Double trele crochet Work as given for main pattern, but use dtr throughout, working ch4 at the beg of each round and ch4 for corner spaces.

variation 3
Psychedelic Work as given for main pattern, working each round in a separate colour, using all 5 yarns.

variation 4
Maze Work as given for main pattern for Rounds 1, 3 and 5 using yarn D, and for Rounds 2 and 4 using yarn C as given for the standard granny square pattern.

variation 5
Half treble crochet Ch5, join into ring with ss. **Round 1:** ch2 (counts as 1htr), 11htr into ring, join with ss into top of ch2. **Round 2:** ch2, 1htr into next st, * 3htr into next st (1st corner worked), 1htr into next 2sts, rep from * twice more, 3htr into last st, join with ss into ch3. **Rounds 3–5:** ch2 (counts as 1htr), * 1htr into each st up to centre st of 1st corner, 3htr into next st, rep from * ending last rep with 1htr into each st to end, join with ss into ch3.

variations

patchwork

see base design on page 129

variation 2

9 squares Work each square as given for
main pattern, using each of the 3 colours for
Round 1, then yarn D for Rounds 2–3. Join
together as per main pattern using yarn D
and use picture as a guide.

variation 3

Mini squares Make 4
squares by working
Round 1 as given for
main pattern in yarn D.
Join these 4 squares
together to make a
larger square by working in ss along the
edges. Repeat this 3 more times to create 4
larger squares made up from the mini
squares. Join the larger squares together to
make an even larger square using yarn B, zig
zagging across between the corner spaces
and ch1 spaces using ch3 and ss to secure.
Join in yarn A. **Round 2:** ch3, work 5tr into
each of the ch sps and ltr in between the ch
sps, rep from * working 3tr into each corner.
Then ss into the ch3.

variation 4

4 squares Work 2 squares in yarn B and 2
squares in yarn A. Join together as per
main pattern using yarn C and the picture
as a guide.

variation 5

Wild colours Work as given for main pattern
for Round 1. **Round 2:** work 1dc into each st,
working 3dc for the corner.. **Round 3:** work
1tr into evey dc and 3tr in each of the corner
sts. Make 4 squares using yarns A, D and B,
using the photo as a guide. Join the squares
together as for main pattern using yarn C,
then work tr around the entire square with
3tr in each corner.

wagon wheels

see base design on page 130

variation 2

Filet edge Work Rounds 1–4 work as given for main pattern. Round 5: ch4 (counts as 1tr and ch1), * sk1, 1tr into next st, ch1, sk1, 2tr, ch3, 2tr into next ch3sp (1st corner worked), ch1, sk1, 1tr into next st, ch1, (1tr, ch1) into next 6 ch1sp, rep from * ending last rep with (1tr, ch1) into 5 ch1sp, join with ss into 3rd of ch4 at beg of round.

variation 4
Cluster centre with solid edging Ch4, join with ss to form a ring. **Rounds 1–3:** work as given for Variation 5. **Rounds 4–5:** work as given for Variation 1.

variation 5
Cluster centre wheel Ch4, join with ss to form a ring. **Round 1:** ch2 (counts as 1tr), 2tr cl into ring, * ch2, 3tr cl into ring, rep from * 4 more times, ch2, join with ss into top of 1st cluster. **Round 2:** ch5 (counts as 1dtr and ch2), 1dtr into ch2sp, * ch2, 1dtr in top of next cl, ch2, 1dtr into next ch2sp, rep from * 4 more times, ch2, ss into 3rd of ch4 at beg of the round. **Round 3:** work as given for Row 3 of main pattern. Fasten off yarn A and join in yarn B. **Round 4:** ch3 (counts as 1tr), 2tr, ch3, 3tr into 1st ch3sp (1st corner worked), * sk next ch1sp (3tr into next ch1sp) twice, (3tr, ch3, 3tr) into next ch3sp, rep from * to end, ss into top of tch. **Round 5:** work as Round 6 of main pattern.

variation 3

Cluster centre with filet edge Ch4, join with ss to form a ring. **Rounds 1–3:** as given for Variation 5. **Rounds 4–5:** as given for Variation 2.

variations

meadow squares

see base design on page 133

variation 2

Puffed violet centre Using yarn A, ch6, join with ss to form a ring. **Round 1:** work as given for main pattern. **Round 2:** * ch1, 1 puff st into next st, ch1, ss into next st, rep from * to end. Break off yarn A and join in yarn D. **Rounds 3–5:** work as given for main pattern. Fasten off.

variation 3

Rose centre Using yarn B, ch12. **Row 1:** 1tr in 4th ch from hook, ch2, 2tr into same ch, * ch1, sk2, work (2 tr, 2 ch, 2tr) into next ch, rep from * to end, turn. **Row 2:** ch1 ss into first ch2 sp, ch3, 6tr in same ch2 sp, * 1dc in ch sp, 7tr in next ch2 sp, rep from * to end. Break off yarn, leaving a long tail, and roll the yarn inward to create rosebud. Using the long tail and a sewing up needle, work a few stitches into the base of flower to secure. Sew in loose ends. Join in yarn D into the base of the rosebud. **Round 1:** * ch2, ss into base of rosebud, rep from * 3 more times to make 4 ch2 loops evenly around the base, working last ss into 1st of 2ch at the beg of the round. **Round 2:** ss into 1st ch2sp, ch3 (counts as 1tr), 2tr into same ch2 cp, ch3, * 3tr into next ch2 sp, ch3, rep from * to end, join with ss into ch3. **Round 3:** work as for Round 4 of main pattern. **Round 4:** work as for Round 5 of main pattern.

variation 4

Pansy centre Using yarn E, ch6, join with ss to form a ring. **Round 1:** as given for main pattern. Break off yarn E and join in yarn A. **Round 2:** ch4, 1dtr into 1st 2sts, ch4, ss into next st, ch4, 1dtr into next 2sts, ch4, ss into next st, * ch3, 1tr into next 2sts, ch3, ss into next st, rep from * to end, join with ss into back loop of ch1. **Round 3:** work as given for Round 3 of main pattern, working into the back of the petals. **Rounds 4–5:** work as given for main pattern.

variation 5

Layered flower centre Using yarn C, ch4, join with ss to form a ring. **Round 1:** ch5 (counts as 1tr and ch2), 1tr into ring, ch2, * 1tr into ring, ch2, rep from * 4 more times, join with ss into 3rd of ch5. **Round 2:** ss into 1st ch2sp, work (1dc, 3tr, 1dc) into 1st and every foll ch2sp to end, join with ss into base of 1dc at beg of the round. Work next round at the back of work to create 6 ch3 loops. **Round 3:** ch3, miss 1st petal, * ss into back of next dc, ch3, rep from * ending last rep with ss into base of ch3. **Round 4:** ss into 1st ch3sp, work (1dc, 5tr, 1dc) into 1st and every foll ch3sp to end, join with ss into base of 1dc at beg of the round. Break off yarn C and join in yarn D. **Rounds 5–7:** work as given for Rounds 3–5 of main pattern.

variations

posy squares

see base design on page 134

variation 2

Three-layer flower Work as given for main pattern. Rounds 1–3 in yarn A, Round 4 in yarn C. **Round 5:** * ch5, Sk 6sts, 1dc into back of next st, rep from * working last dc into base of ch5 at beg of the row. Break off yarn C and join in yarn D. **Round 6:** * ch1, 7tr into 1st ch5 loop, ch1, ss into top of 1dc, rep from * to end, join with ss into 1dc at beg of round. **Round 7:** as Round 6 of main pattern. **Rounds 8–9:** as Round 7 of main pattern. Fasten off.

variation 3

Daffodil Using yarn E, ch4, join with ss to form a ring. **Round 1:** ch2 (counts as 1htr), 11htr into ring. **Round 2:** * ch1, work (1htr, 1tr, 1htr) into next st (1st petal base made), ch1, ss into next st, rep from * ending last rep with ss into ch1. **Round 3:** ch3, sk 1st petal base, 1dc into back of next htr in Row 1, * sk next petal base, sk next htr of row 1, 1dc into next htr of row 1, rep from * ending last rep with ss into base of ch3. **Round 4:** ch1, work (1htr, 1tr, 1dtr, 1tr, 1htr) into 1st ch3 loop, ch1, 1dc into next st, * ch1, work (1htr, 1tr, 1dtr, 1tr, 1htr) into next ch3 loop, ch1, 1dc into next st, rep from * to end. **Round 5:** work as Round 6 of main pattern. **Rounds 6–7:** work as Round 7 of main pattern in yarn B for square. Fasten off.

variation 4

Offset petal flower Using yarn B, ch4, join with ss to form a ring. **Round 1:** ch5 (counts as 1tr and ch2), * 1tr into ring, ch2, rep from * 4 more times, join with ss into 3rd of ch5. **Round 2:** work (1dc, 3tr, 1dc) into next and every foll ch2sp to end, join with ss into back of 1dc at beg of round. Work next round at the back of flower. **Round 3:** ss into back of next 3sts, * ch3, sk4, ss into back of next st, rep from * ending last rep with ss into base of ch3. **Round 4:** work (1dc, 5tr, 1dc) into next and every foll ch3sp to end, join with ss into back of 1dc at beg of round. **Round 5:** work as Round 6 of main pattern. **Rounds 6–7:** work as Round 7 of main pattern in yarn B for square. Fasten off.

variation 5

Geranium Using yarn F, ch4, join with ss to form a ring. **Round 1:** * ch2, 2tr into ring, ch2, ss into ring (1st petal worked), rep from * 3 more times, join with ss into base of ch2. Work next round at the back of the flower. **Round 2:** ch1, ss to back 1st st, * ch2, dc into back of the middle st of next petal, rep from * to end. **Round 3:** ch2, sk. Round 3: * ch3, 4dtr, ch3 into 1st ch2 loop, ss into next st, rep from * to end. Fasten off yarn F and join in yarn B. **Rounds 4–6:** work as Rounds 5–7 of main pattern.

variations

claude

see base design on page 137

variation 1

Blossom square Using yarn H, ch3, join with ss to form a ring. **Round 1:** ch2 (counts as 1htr), 7htr into ring, join with ss to ch2. **Round 2:** ch3 (counts as 1tr), 2tr into base of ch, ch1, * 3tr into next st, ch1, rep from * to end, join with ss into top of ch3, turn. Fasten off yarn H and join in yarn B. **Round 3:** ss into ch1sp, ch3 (counts as 1tr), 1tr, ch3, 2tr into same sp, * 2tr, ch3, 2tr into next ch1sp, rep from * 5 more time, join with ss into top of ch3, turn. **Round 4:** ss into 1st 2sts, work (1dc, 3tr, 1dc) into next and each ch2sp to end, join with ss into base of 1dc. Fasten off yarn J. Join in yarn J to tip of 1st petal with ss. **Round 5:** * ch6, ss to tip of next petal, rep from * to end. Work as per main pattern from Round 4 to end.

variation 2

Daisy Using yarn J, ch4, join with ss into a ring. **Round 1:** ch1 (counts as 1dc), 7dc into ring, join with ss into ch1. Fasten off yarn J, join in yarn A. **Round 2:** * ch10, ss into 3rd ch from hook to make picot, 1tr into each of the remaining ch7, ss into next st, rep from * to ending last rep with ss into base of ch10. Complete pattern as given for Variation 4 using yarn F.

variation 3

Shamrock Work as given for main pattern, working in shades of green to create a four-leaf clover effect.

variation 5

Dog rose Using yarn H ch5, join with ss to form a ring. Fasten off yarn H and join in yarn A. **Round 1:** ch3, * 2tr cl into ring, ch1, rep from * 7 more times, join with ss into top of ch3. Fasten off yarn A and join in yarn G. **Round 2:** ch1, work (1dc, 3tr, 1dc) into next and every foll ch1sp, join with ss into ch1. **Round 3:** ch1, 1dc into same place, * ch5, 1dc into centre st of next 3tr, rep from * to end, join with ss into 1dc. **Round 4:** ss into 1st ch5sp, ch3 (counts as 1tr), 2tr, ch3, 3tr into same sp (1st corner worked), * ch1, 3tr into next ch5sp, ch1, (3tr, ch3, 3tr) into next ch5sp, rep from * twice more, ch1, 3tr into last ch5sp, ch1, join with ss into ch3. **Round 5:** work as given for Round 6 of main pattern.

let it snow

see base design on page 138

variation 2

Hexagonal snowflake Using yarn B, ch4, join with ss to form a ring. **Round 1:** ch1 (counts as 1dc), 5dc into ring, join with ss into ch1.

Round 2: ch5 (counts as 1tr and ch2), 1tr into same st, * work (1tr, ch2, 1tr) in next st, rep from * to end, ss into 3rd of ch5. **Round 3:** ss into 1st ch2sp, ch3 (counts as 1tr), 1tr, ch3, 2tr into same sp, work * (2tr, ch3, 2tr) into next ch2sp, rep from * to end, join with ss into ch3. **Round 4:** ss into next 2sts and ch3sp, ch3 (counts as 1tr), 2tr, ch3, 3tr into same sp, * work (3tr, ch3, 3tr) into next ch3sp, ch1, rep from * to end, join with ss into ch3. **Round 5:** ss into next 2sts and into ch3sp, ch3 (counts as 1tr), work (3tr, ch2, 4tr, ch2) into same sp, * work (3tr, ch2, 4tr, ch2) in next ch3sp, rep from * to end, join with ss into ch3. Fasten off yarn B and join in yarn C to any of the ch2 sp's. **Round 6:** ch1 (counts as 1dc), 1dc, ch2, 2dc into same sp, * 1htr into next 4sts, 3tr into next ch2sp, 1htr into next 2sts, work (2dc, ch2, 2dc) into next ch2sp, rep from * to end, join with ss into ch1. **Round 7:** ss into 1st st, ch3, (1tr, ch3, 2tr) in ch sp, * 1tr in each of next 13 sts, 2tr 2ch, 2tr into corner, rep from * 6 more times, 1tr in each of next 13 sts, join with ss into ch3.

variation 3

Hoopla snow Work as given for main pattern using hoopla yarn.

variation 4

Flake Using yarn B, work Rounds 1–5 as given for Variation 2. Fasten off yarn B and join in yarn C to any ch2sp's. **Round 6:** ch2, 1dc, * ch8, 2dc into next ch sp, rep from * 6 more times, join with ss into ch2. **Round 7:** ch3, 1tr into dc of prev round, * 10tr into ch8sp, 1tr into next 2sts, rep from * 6 times, join with ss into ch3. **Round 8:** ch3, 1tr into same ch sp, * work 1tr into each of the next 8sts, 2tr into next sp, rep from * to end, join with a ss into ch3. Fasten off.

variation 5

Granny edge Using yarn B, work Rounds 1–5 as given for Variation 2. Fasten off yarn B and join in yarn E to any ch2sp. **Round 6:** ch3, (2dc, ch2, 3dc), * ch1, sk1, 3dc in between the next 2dc, ch1, sk1, 3dc in the next ch sp, ch1, sk1, 3dc into next sp, ch1, sk1, ss into next sp, ch1, sk1, 3dc into next st, ch1, sk1, 3dc into next sp, ch1, sk1, 3dc into next sp, (3dc, 2ch, 3dc) into next st, rep from * 3 more times, join with a ss into ch3. **Round 7:** ss into next 2sts, ch3, (1dc, ch2, 2dc), ch1, * work 3dc, 1ch into the next 7 ch sp, (3dc, 2ch, 3dc) into corner, rep from * 3 more times, join with ss into ch3. Fasten off.

bullion in the round

see base design on page 141

variation 2

Around the round Using yarn B, ch6, join with ss to form a ring. **Round 1:** ch3, 7BS into a ring, join with ss into top of tch, hide ch3 behind first and last BS. Fasten off yarn B and join in yarn C. **Round 2:** ch3, 2BS into each st to end, 1BS into top of tch from prev round, join with ss into tch. Fasten off.

variation 3

Using yarn C, ch6, join with ss to form a ring. **Round 1:** ch3, 10BS into a ring, join with ss into top of tch. **Round 2:** ch3, 2tr into each st to end, join with ss into top of tch. **Round 3:** ch3, 2BS into 1st st, * 1BS into next st, 2BS into next st, rep from * 8 more times, 1BS into last st, join with ss into top of tch. Fasten off.

variation 4

Square Using yarn A, ch6, join with ss to form a ring. **Round 1:** work as given for main pattern. Break off yarn A and join in yarn C. **Round 2:** ch3, 2BS into each st to end, join with ss into top of tch. Break off yarn C and join in yarn B. **Round 3:** ch3, * 1BS into the next 5sts, then (3BS, ch3, 3BS) into the next st, rep from * 3 more times, join with ss into top of tch. Fasten off.

variation 5

Daisy Using yarn B, ch5, join with ss to form a ring. **Round 1:** ch1, 9 dc into ring, join with ss into 1 ch at beg of the round. **Round 2:** ch5, ss into base of ch, * 1 dc into next 2sts, ch5, ss into dc just worked, rep from * 4 more times, 1 dc into last st, makes 5 loops – do not break off yarn. Join in yarn A. **Round 3:** ch1, (1 dc, 5BS, 1 dc) into 1st loop, * (1dc, 5BS, 1dc) into next loop, rep from * to end. Join in yarn B. **Round 4:** ch1, * 1dc into dc from prev round, work the foll around 1st petal (2dc in between dc and BS, 2dc in between each BS, 2dc in between last BS and dc), rep from * working around each petal. Fasten off.

spinning wheels

see base design on page 142

variation 2

Flat petal square Work as given for main pattern working Rounds 1–2 in yarn A and Rounds 3–4 in yarn E.

variation 3

Granny edge Work as given for main pattern working Rounds 1–2 in yarn F. Work next round at the back of work. Join in yarn A.

Round 3: * ch3, dc to back of ss between petals, rep from * to ending last rep with ss into base of ch3. **Round 4:** ch3 (counts as 1tr), 2tr, ch3 into 1st ch3 loop (1st corner worked), ch1, * 3tr, ch3 into next ch3 loop, ch1, rep from * twice more, join with ss to top of ch3. **Round 5:** ss into next 2sts and into 1st ch3sp, ch3, 2tr, ch3, 3tr into same sp (1st corner worked) ch1, * 3tr, into next ch1sp, ch1, 3tr, ch3, 3tr into next ch3sp, ch1, rep from * twice more, ch1, 3tr into last ch1sp, ch1, join with ss to top of ch3. **Round 6:** work pattern as given for granny square, with (3tr, ch3, 3tr) into corner ch3sp, and 3tr into each ch1 sp, ending with ch1 and ss into ch3. Repeat last round to required size.

variation 4

Solid square edge Work as given for main pattern, working Rounds 1–2 in yarn A. Fasten off yarn A and join in yarn B. **Round 3:** ch3, 1tr into 1st 2sts, * (3tr, ch3, 3tr) into 1st ch3sp, work 1tr into each of the next (3tr, ch1sp, 3tr), ch1sp **, (3tr), rep from * ending last rep at **, ss into top of ch3.

variation 5

Hexagon edge Work as given for main pattern working Rounds 1–2 in yarn B. Fasten off yarn B and join in yarn D to centre st of petal. **Round 3:** ch1, 1dc into centre st, * ch10, 1dc centre of next petal, rep from * to end, join with ss into ch1. **Round 4:** ch3 (counts as 1tr), work (2tr, ch1, 3tr, ch1, 3tr) into 1st ch10 sp, * ch3, work (3tr, ch1) 3 times into next ch10sp, rep from * ending last rep with ch3, join with ss into ch3.

variations

climbing roses

see base design on page 145

variation 1

Tropical square Work as given for main pattern, using yarn J for Rounds 1–3, yarn H for Rounds 4–5 and yarn E for Round 6 onwards.

variation 3

Framed filet Work as given for main pattern for Rounds 1–6, using yarn B for the first layer, yarn F for the second layer, and yarn H for the square. **Round 7:** work as per Variation 1. **Round 8:** work 1 tr into each st and ch sp, make corner as before. **Round 9:** work as in main pattern.

variation 2

Climbing roses Work as given for main pattern for Rounds 1–6, using yarn H for Rounds 1–3, yarn E for Rounds 4–5 and yarn D for Round 6 onwards.

variation 4

Honeysuckle Work as per Variation 2, using a row of dc for Rounds 8 and 10.

variations

doilies

see base design on page 146

variation 2

Star doily Using yarn C, ch9, join with ss to form a ring.
Round 1: ch3 (counts as 1tr), 15tr into ring, join with ss into tch. **Round 2:** ch6 (counts as 1dtr and ch2), 1dtr into next st, ch2, 1dtr into next st, ch2 rep from * to end, join with ss to 4th ch of ch6. **Round 3:** ch4 (counts as 1dtr), 3dtr into ch2sp. *4dtr into next ch sp, rep from *to end, join with ss in to top of tch. **Round 4:** ch3 (counts as 1tr), 1tr into same st, ch4, sk3, 2tr in between next 2sts, * ch4 **, sk4, 2tr in between next 2 dtr, rep from * ending last rep at **, join with ss into top of tch. **Round 5:** ch3 (counts as 1tr), 1tr in between next 2sts, ch3, 2tr into same place, 1dc into ch4sp, * work (2tr, ch3, 2tr) in between next 2sts, 1dc into next ch4sp, rep from * to end, join with ss into top of ch3. Fasten off.

variation 3

Simple dinky doily Using yarn E, ch8, join with ss to form a ring.
Round 1: ch3 (counts as 1tr), 2tr cl into ring, ch2, * 3tr cl into ring, ch2, rep from * 6 more times, join with ss into ch3. **Round 2:** work as given for Round 2, Variation 1. **Round 3:** ch3 (counts as 1tr), 1tr, ch3, 2tr into ch2sp, 1dc into next ch2sp, * (2tr, ch3, 2tr) into next ch2sp, 1dc into next ch2sp, rep from * to end, join with ss into ch3.

variation 4

Mini doily Using yarn B, ch4, join with ss to form a ring.
Round 1: work as given for main pattern in tr, with ch5 at beg of round. **Round 2:** work as given for main pattern, with ch3 at beg of round, turn at the end of this round. **Round 3:** ch1, ss into 1st st, 1dc into next ch2sp, * ch4, sk1, dtr3tog, ch4, 1dc into next ch2sp, rep from * to end, join with ss into dc at beg of round, turn. **Round 4:** MP, * 4dc into ch4sp, 1dc into top of dtr3tog, MP, 1dc into top of dtr3tog, 4dc into ch4sp, 1dc into next st, MP, rep from * to end, join with ss into base of 1st picot.

variation 5

Cluster stitch doily Using yarn F, ch10, join with ss to form a ring.
Round1: ch3 (counts as 1tr), 2tr cl into ring, ch2, * 3tr cl into ring, ch2, rep from * 8 more times, join with ss into ch3. **Round 2:** ch3 (counts as 1tr), 2tr cl into 1st ch2sp, *ch5, 3tr into next ch2sp, rep from * 8 more times, ch5, join with ss into ch3. **Round 3:** ch3 (counts as 1tr), work (2tr cl, ch3, 3tr cl) into 1st ch5sp, ch3, * (3tr cl, ch3, 3tr cl) into next ch5sp, ch3, rep from * to end, join with ss into top of 1st cluster. **Round 4:** * 5tr into 1st ch3sp, 1dc into next ch3sp, rep from * to end. Fasten off.

variations

maude

see main design on page 149

variation 2
Two-colour Work as given for main pattern.
Rounds 1–3: using yarn A. **Rounds 4–6:**
using yarn B.

variation 4
Alternating colours Work as given for main
pattern. **Rounds 1, 3 and 5:** using yarn A.
Rounds 2 and 4: using yarn B. **Round 6:**
using yarn B, ch2, 1htr into next 3sts, 1dc
into next 9sts, 1htr into next 4sts, * 3tr, 2ch,
3tr all into next st, 1 htr into next 4sts,
1dc into next 9sts, 1htr into next 4sts, rep
from * 3 more times, join with a ss into top
of ch2. Fasten off.

variation 3
Multicolour Work as given for main pattern.
Round 1: using yarn A. **Round 2:** using yarn
B. **Rounds 3:** using yarn C. **Round 4:** using
yarn D. **Rounds 5–6:** using yarn E.

variation 5
Hoopla! Work as given for main pattern
using hoopla yarn and 12mm hook.

colour work

Now you'll have the chance to play with
colour every stitch of the way. Experiment
with bold designs and unusual shapes as you
work hues and shades into each project. There
is no limit to what you can do – just make sure
you've got enough wool!

vintage stripes

Main pattern: using yarn A, ch28+3ch for turning.

Row 1: 1tr in 4th ch from hook, sk2, * 3tr into next ch, sk2, rep from * ending, 2tr into last ch, turn.

Row 2: ch3, sk2, 3tr, into 1st sp, * sk3, 3tr into next sp, rep from * to end, work 1tr into top of ch3, turn.

Row 3: ch3, 1tr into 1st sp, * sk3, 3tr into next sp, rep from * 6 more times, sk3, 2tr into top of ch3, turn.

Rows 2–3 form the pattern; repeat to required length. Fasten off.

materials

- 4mm hook
- Sublime Baby Cashmere Merino Silk DK in 04 Gooseberry (A), 246 Puffin (B), 01 Piglet (C), 159 Little Miss Plum (D)

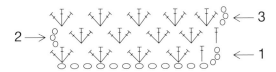

see other variations on page 194

variation 1

Two-colour stripes Work as given for main pattern, working odd rows in yarn A and even rows in yarn B. Fasten off.

cornered

Main pattern: using yarn A, ch4, join with ss to form a ring.

Row 1: ch3 (counts as 1st tr), 2tr, ch3, 3tr into ring, turn.

Row 2: ch3, sk1, 1tr into next 2sts, (2tr, ch3, 2tr) into ch3 sp, 1tr into next 3 sts, turn.

Row 3: ch3, sk1, 1tr into each st to ch3 sp, (2tr, ch3, 2tr) into ch3 sp, 1tr into each st to end, turn.

Row 3 forms pattern; repeat to required length.

materials

- 4.5mm hook
- Rowan All Seasons Cotton in Jacuzzi (A), Damson (B), Blush (C), Hedge (D), String (E)

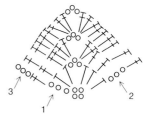

see other variations on page 195

variation 1

Striped corner square Work as given for main pattern, working Rows 1–2 in yarn B and Row 3 in yarn C. Keeping pattern correct, work in stripe sequence using the picture as a guide.

spiked

Main pattern: using yarn A, ch18+1 for turning.

Row 1: 1dc into 2nd ch from hook, 1dc to end, turn.

Rows 2–3: ch1, 1dc into each st to end, turn. Fasten off yarn A and join in yarn B.

Row 4: ch1, 1dc into 1st st, * work 1 spike st (sp st by inserting hook 1 row below and working dc as normal * 1dc in next st, rep from * to end, turn.

Row 5: work as Row 2. Break off yarn B and join in yarn A.

Row 6: work as Row 4.

Rows 7–9: work as Rows 1–3. Repeat Rows 1–9 to set pattern.

materials

■ 4mm hook
■ Sublime Baby Cashmere Merino Silk DK in Teddy Red (A), Caterpillar (B), Seesaw (C), Ragdoll (D)

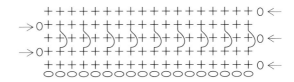

see other variations on page 196

variation 1

Bird's foot clusters Using yarn C, ch18+1 and work Rows 1–3 as given for main pattern. Fasten off yarn C and join in yarn B. **Row 4:** 1dc into next 2 sts, * work bird's foot cluster (BFC) as follows: Insert hook into stitch to the right of the st below, yarn over, pull loop through, insert hook into st below on row below, YOH, pull loop through, insert hook into st to the left of st on row below, YOH, pull loop through, YOH, pull loop through all the loops on hook to close cluster, 1dc into next 3sts, rep from * to end. **Rows 5–7:** work as Rows 2–3. **Row 8:** work as Row 4, working BFC on right-side facing rows.

evening sunset

Main pattern: using yarn A, ch5, join with ss to form a ring.

Round 1: ch3 (counts as 1tr), 11tr into ring, join with ss into ch3. Fasten off yarn A and join in yarn B.

Round 2: ss in between 1st and 2nd sts, ch3 (counts as 1tr), 1tr into same sp, work 2tr in between next and every st foll to end, working last 2sts in between last st and ch3, join with ss into ch3.Fasten off yarn B and join in yarn C.

Round 3: ss in between 1st and 2nd sts, ch3 (counts as 1tr), 2tr into same sp, work 3tr in between next and every foll st to end, working last 3 sts in between last st and ch3, join with ss into ch3.

Fasten off yarn C and join in yarn D.

Round 4: ss into next 2sts and in between next 2sts, ch3 (counts as 1tr), 2tr, ch3, 3tr into same sp (1st corner worked), * (sk3, 3tr in between next 2 sts) twice **, sk3, work (3tr, ch3, 3tr) in between next 2 sts, rep from * ending last rep at **, join with ss into ch3.

Project notes: Cushion. Make 12 squares using 4 colours. Make 2 squares of each colour combination and join at stage 4 of the pattern, using the 'on-the-go' method. For the back piece of the cover, make a chain.the length of the cushion front and work in granny stripes. With wrong sides together, join 2

sides using double crochet, inserting cushion pad before crocheting up the last side.

materials

- 4mm hook
- King Cole Bamboo Cotton DK in Yellow (A), Aqua (B), Red (C), White (D), Plum (E), Green (F)

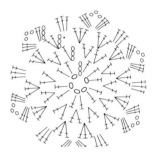

see other variations on page 197

variation 1

Reverse colours Work as given for main pattern, using the colours in reverse order.

candy

Main Pattern: using yarn A, ch2.

Row 1: 3dc into 2nd ch from hook, turn.

Row 2: ch1, 1dc into 1st 2st, 2dc into last, turn.

Row 3: ch1, 1dc into 1st 3st, 2dc into last, turn. Fasten off yarn A and join in yarn B.

Row 4: ch1, 1dc into each st to last st, 2dc into last st.

Repeat last row until 20 sts, changing colour every 3rd row.

Next row: ch1, 1dc into each st to end, turn.

Next row (dec): ch1, sk1, 1dc into each st to last st, sk1, 1dc into ch1.

Repeat last row until 2 sts remain.

Next row: ch1, dc2tog. Fasten off.

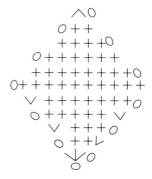

> **materials**
>
> ■ 5mm hook
> ■ Rowan All Seasons Cotton in 241 Damson (A), 242 Blush (B), 246 Hedge (C), 239 Jacuzzi (D)

see other variations on page 198

variation 1

Single colour stripes Work as given for main pattern, working each row in different colour yarns. Rows 1–3 in yarn A, Rows 4–7 in yarn B and Rows 8–12 in yarn C. Work the remaining increase rows in yarn A, and then reverse the stripe for decrease rows.

polka

Main pattern: using yarn B, ch5, join with ss to form a ring.

Round 1: ch2 (counts as 1htr), 11htr into ring, join with ss into ch2.

Round 2: ch2 (counts as 1htr), 1htr in 1st st, 2htr in each st to end, join with ss into ch2.

Round 3: ch2 (counts as 1htr), 1htr into 1st st, * 1htr into next st, 2htr into next, rep from * to last st, 1htr into last st, join with ss into ch2. Fasten off yarn B and join in yarn A.

Round 4: ch3 (counts as 1htr and ch1), 1htr into same st (1st corner worked), * 1htr into next 8 sts, work (1tr, ch2, 1tr) into next st, rep from * twice more, 1htr into last 8 sts, join with ss into 2nd of ch3.

Rounds 5–6: ss into 1st corner, ch3 (counts as 1tr), work (1tr, ch3, 2tr) into same sp, * work 1 htr into each st to next corner, work (3tr, ch3, 3tr) into next corner sp, rep from * twice more, then work 1htr into each st to end, join with ss into ch2. Fasten off.

materials

- 4mm hook
- Sublime Baby Cashmere Merino Silk DK in 194 Seesaw (A), 243 Little Miss Plum (B), 245 Caterpillar (C), 244 Ragdoll (D), 01 Piglet (E)

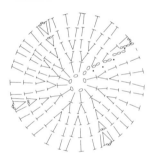

see other variations on page 199

variation 1

Puffed centre Using yarn C, begin and work Round 1 as in main pattern. **Round 2:** ch3, work 23 double crochet OVER Round 1, into the original ch4 ring. **Round 3:** ch3 (counts as 1htr and ch1), 1htr into same st (1st corner worked), * 1htr into next 6 sts, work (1tr, ch2, 1tr) into next st, rep from * twice more, 1htr into last 6 sts, join with ss into 2nd of ch3. **Rounds 4–5:** using yarn A, work as in main pattern.

wedges

Notes:
FPDTR=front post treble crochet
FPTRTR=front post double treble crochet
FPQUARDTR=front post triple treble crochet

Main pattern: using yarn A, ch16.

Row 1: 1tr in 4th ch from hook, 1tr in each st to end, turn.

Row 2: ch3, 1tr in each st to end, turn.

Row 3: ch3, * sk3, work (1FPdtr, 1FPtrtr, 1FPquadtr) around stem of next st on row below, 1tr in top of same st, rep from * to last st, 1tr, turn.

Rows 2–3 form the pattern.; repeat to required length, ending on Row 2. Fasten off.

materials

- 4mm hook
- King Cole Bamboo Cotton in Opal (A), Cobalt (B), Cream (C)

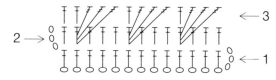

see other variations on page 200

variation 1
Colour variation Work as given for main pattern, with Rows 1–2 in yarn B and Row 3 in yarn A.

tweedy square

Main pattern: using yarn A, ch26.

Row 1: 1dc into 2nd ch from hook, * 1dc into next st, rep from * to end, turn.

Row 2: ch1, 1dc into 1st st, * ch2, sk2, 1dc into next st, repeat from * to end, turn.

Row 3: ch3, 1tr into 1st st, * sk2, 3tr into next st, repeat from * ending last rep with, 2tr, turn.

Rows 2–3 form the pattern; repeat until 16 rows have been worked.

materials

- 4mm hook
- Debbie Bliss Cotton DK in Brown (A), Beige (B), Grass Green (C), Light Turquoise (D), Dark Turquoise (E)

see other variations on page 201

variation 1

Mixed stripes Work as given for main pattern, working Rows 1–6 in yarn B, Row 7 in yarn A, Row 8 in yarn B and Row 9 in yarn A. Rows 1–9 form stripe sequence while keeping pattern. Repeat stripe to required length.

knot

Main pattern: using yarn A, ch12.

Row 1: 1dc into 2nd ch from hook, 1dc in each st to end, turn.

Row 2: ch1, 1dc in next st, * 1dtr in next st, 1dc in next st, rep from * to end, finishing on dc, turn.

Row 3: ch1, 1dc in each st to end, turn.

Rows 2–3 form the pattern. Repeat for a further 9 rows.

```
    + + + + + + + + + +
2 → 0+ T + T + T + T + T +  0   ← 3
    + + + + + + + + + +0      ← 1
    o o o o o o o o o o
```

---

variation 1

see other variations on page 202

Offset knot Using yarn B, ch12. **Rows 1–3:** work as per main pattern. **Row 4:** ch1, 1dc in each of next 2sts, * 1dtr in next st, 1dc in next st, rep from * to last 2sts, 1dc into last 2sts, turn. **Row 5:** work as Row 3. Rows 2–5 form the pattern. Repeat to required length.

box

Main pattern: using yarn A, ch6.

Row 1: 1tr into 4th ch from hook, 1tr each into next 2 sts, turn. Break off yarn A and join in yarn B.

Row 2: ch6, 1tr into 4th ch from hook, 1tr into next 2ch, sk2, ss into top of ch3, ch3, work 3tr around stem of st and 1tr into 1st ch, turn. Break off yarn B and join in yarn C.

Next row (increasing): ch6, 1tr in 4th ch from hook, and in next 2 ch, * sk3, ss into top of next ch3, ch3, work 4tr around stem of next st. Break off yarn C and join in yarn D. Keeping stripe sequence correct, repeat last row 6 more times.

Row 7 (decreasing): ss into next 3sts and top of ch3, * ch3, 1tr into ch3 of prev row, sk3sts, ss into top of next ch3, rep from * to end, turn. Repeat last row until square is formed.

Project notes: Pot holder. Crochet 2 blocks of main pattern. With wrong sides facing, dc together with contrasting yarn. Make a hanging loop by making a rectangle (see Chapter 4: Shaped motifs) and insert it into the corner of the piece. Make a pretty, loopy edge by working * ch5, dc into next. Repeat from * along to end.

materials

- 4mm hook
- Rowan Wool Cotton in Coffee (A), Mocha (B), Elf (C), Antique (D)

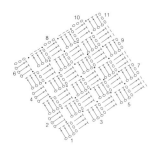

see other variations on page 203

variation 1

Block stripe Work as given for main pattern, with 2 rows of each colour for a bold stripe effect, working 6 increase rows before switching to decrease rows to form a square.

mary

Main pattern: using yarn A, ch14+2ch.

Row 1: 1dc into 3rd ch from hook, 1dc into next st, (1htr into next ch) twice, (1tr into next ch) twice, (1dtr into next ch) 3 times, (1tr into next ch) twice, (1htr into next ch) twice, 1dc into last st, turn.

Row 2: ch4, 1dtr into 1st st, (1tr into next 2 sts), (1htr into next 2sts), (1dc into next 3sts), (1htr into next 2sts), (1tr into next 2sts), (1dtr into last 2sts), turn. Fasten off yarn A and join in yarn B.

Row 3: ch1, 1dc into 1st 2 sts, work (1htr into next st) twice, (1tr into next st) twice, (1dtr into next st) 3 times, (1tr into next st) twice, (1htr into next st) twice, 1dc into last st, turn.

Rows 2–3 form the pattern; repeat, working 2 rows in each colour.

Project notes: Cushion cover.
Work as given for main pattern, using a 5mm hook and Debbie Bliss Cashmerino Aran, work as per main pattern. Use a foundation chain of 56+1 for turning.

materials

- 4mm hook
- Debbie Bliss Rialto DK in Duck Egg (A), Gold (B), Apple (C), Teal (D), Red (E)

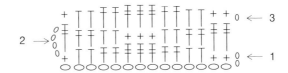

see other variations on page 204

variation 1

Broken waves Using yarn A, ch14+2 ch. **Row 1:** work as per main pattern. Fasten off yarn A and join in yarn E. **Row 2:** ch1, sk1, 1dc into each st to end, turn. Fasten off yarn E and join in yarn C. **Row 3:** work as Row 2 of main pattern. Fasten off yarn C and join in yarn E. **Row 4:** work as Row 2 of this variation.

rainbow

Main pattern: *make a magic circle (see page 19).*

Round 1: * 1ch, 1dc, 1htr, 2tr in ring, remove hook but do not cut yarn, leaving a long loop, join in yarn B, repeat from *, rep with yarn C and D. Pull tail to close magic circle.

Round 2: with yarn A, * 2tr in 1st st, 1tr in next st, 2tr in next st, 1tr in next st, rep from * with B, C and D.

Round 3: with yarn A, * ch2, 1tr in next tr, sk1, 2tr in each of the next 2 sts, sk1, 1tr, rep from * with B, C and D.

Round 4: with yarn A, * 2tr, ch2, 2tr into ch sp, sk1, ch1, work (2tr in next st) 3 times, rep from * with B, C and D.

Round 5: with yarn A, * ch1, 3tr, ch2, 3tr in ch2 sp, sk2, ch1, 2tr in ch1sp, sk2, ch1, 1htr, 1dc in ch sp, sk2, ch1, 1dc, ss into last ch1 sp, rep from * with B, C and D.

materials

- 4mm hook
- Sublime Baby Cashmere Merino Silk DK in Ragdoll (A), Cheeky (B), Caterpillar (C), Puzzle (D), Puffin (F)

variation 1

see other variations on page 205

Solid spiral granny square Work Rounds 1–2 as given for main pattern. **Round 3:** with yarn A, * ch2, 2tr into 1st st, 1tr into next 5sts, rep from * with B, C and D. **Round 4:** with yarn A, * ch1, 2tr, ch2, 2tr in ch sp, 1tr into each of next 7sts, rep from * with B, C and D. **Round 5:** with yarn A, * work 1tr into next st, 1htr into next st, 1dc into next st, ss into next st, fasten off, rep from * with colours B, C and D.

intarsia

Main pattern: Using yarn A, ch11, join in yarn B and ch11. Work from chart using htr throughout and 2 turning chains, changing colours as shown in chart.

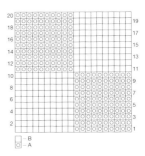

materials

- 4mm hook
- Debbie Bliss Rialto in Bark (A), Sage (B), Emerald (C), Baby Pink (D), Spruce (E), Grey (F), Brown (G), Brick Red (H), White (I)

see other variations on page 206

variation 1

Checks Make 4 wrappings of yarn A and 4 wrappings of yarn C. Using yarn A, ch21. Work from chart in dc and 1 turning chain, joining in colours and working as shown in chart.

christmas tree

Main pattern: make 2 small balls
of yarn A and wrappings of yarns B
and C. Using yarn A, ch29.

Work from chart using dc
throughout and 1 turning chain,
joining in yarns B and C, and
changing colours as shown in chart.

materials

- 4mm hook
- Debbie Bliss Rialto in Ecru
  (A), Brown (B), Moss (C),
  Deep Rose (D), Apple (E),
  Aqua (F), Pink (G)

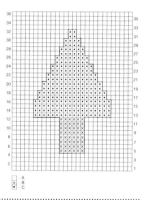

see other variations on page 207

variation 1

Tree with baubles Work as given for main pattern, working a bobble at each end of the
tree on Rows 11, 15, 19, 23 and 27. Then, work a bobble over 2 stitches at the very top of
the tree, using yarns D, E, F and G.

baby's blocks

Main pattern: make 3 wrappings of yarn A and 2 wrappings of yarn B. Using yarn A, ch19.

Work in dc as the chart using the intarsia method and ch1 at the beginning of every row.

Project notes: Toy block. Make one of each of the squares. Sew together to form a cube and stuff using a cube of foam or stuffing.

materials

- 4mm hook
- King Cole Bamboo Cotton in Oyster (A), Yellow (B), Aqua (C), Moss (D), Rose (E), Cobalt (F), Damson (G)

see other variations on page 208

variation 1

Big letter B Make 3 wrappings of yarn A and 2 wrappings of yarn C. Using yarn A, ch19. Work in dc as shown on the chart, using the intarsia method and ch1 at the beginning of every row.

vintage stripes

see base design page on 165

variation 2

Four-colour stripes Work as given for main pattern working Row 1 in yarn A, Row 2 in yarn B, Row 3 in yarn C and Row 4 in yarn D. Keeping pattern correct, work stripe sequence as set to required length. Fasten off.

variation 4

Puff stitch stripe Using yarn B, work pattern as given for Variation 3, working puff st and stripe pattern as per Variation 1 throughout.

variation 3

Cluster stripe Using yarn C, ch28+3 ch for turning. **Row 1:** 2tr cl into 4th ch from hook, ch2, sk2, * 3tr cl into next ch, ch2, sk2, rep from * to end, turn. **Row 2:** ch3, 3tr cl into 1st ch2sp, ch2, * 3tr cl into next ch2 sp, rep from * ending last rep with 3tr cl into top of ch3, turn. Repeat Row 2 to required length. Fasten off.

variation 5

Combinations Using yarn D, work Rows 1–3 as given for main pattern. Fasten off yarn D and join in yarn B. **Row 4:** ch1, 1dc into top of 1st cluster, * 2dc into next ch2sp, 1dc into next cluster, rep from * to end working 1dc into ch3, turn. Rows 1–4 form the pattern. Repeat to required length. Fasten off.

cornered

see base design on page 166

variation 2

Rainbow corner square Work as given for main pattern, working each row in a contrasting colour to create a rainbow effect.

variation 4

Half treble crochet Using yarn E, work as given for Variation 3, with ch2 for turning, change each dc to htr and each htr to tr.

variation 3

Double crochet corner block Using yarn B, ch4, join with ss to form a ring. **Row 1:** ch1, 3dc, 1htr, 3dc into ring, turn. **Row 2:** ch1, 1dc into each dc, work (1dc, 1htr, 1dc) into next st (corner worked), 1dc into each st to end, turn. **Row 3:** ch1, sk1, 1dc into each dc, work (1dc, 1htr, 1dc) into next st (corner worked), 1dc into each dc to end, turn. Repeat last row to required size.

variation 5

Double treble crochet Using yarn D, work as given for main pattern, with ch4 for turning, change each tr to dtr and work ch4 for corner ch sp.

variations

spiked

see base design on page 169

variation 2
Eyelash spike stitch
Using yarn C, ch18+1 and work Rows 1–3 as given for main pattern. Fasten off yarn C and join in yarn A. **Row 4:** ch1, 1dc into 1st st, * 1 sp st on row below, 1sp st on 2 rows below, 1sp st on 3 rows below, 1sp on 2 rows below, 1sp st on 1 row below, 1dc into next st, rep from * twice more, 1dc into last st, turn.
Rows 5–7: work as Rows 1–3. Repeat Rows 4–7.

variation 3
Rake stitch Using yarn D, ch17 and work Rows 1–3 as given for main pattern. Fasten off yarn D and join in yarn C. **Row 4:** work 1 sp st into next 5 sts 3 rows below, 1tr into next 5 sts, 1 sp st into next 5 sts 3 rows below, turn. **Rows 5–6:** work as Rows 2–3. Repeat Rows 1–6.

variation 4
Ascending spikes
Using yarn C, ch18+1 and work Rows 1–3 as given for main pattern. Fasten off yarn C and join in yarn A.
Row 4: ch1, 1dc into 1st st, * 1sp st into row below, 1sp into 2 rows below, 1sp st into 3 rows below, 1sp st into 4 rows below 1dc into next st, rep from * twice more, 1dc into last st, turn. **Rows 5–7:** work as Rows 1–3. Repeat Rows 4–7.

variation 5
Larksfoot crochet
Using yarn A, ch18+1.
Row 1: 1tr in 4th ch from hook, 1tr into next st, * ch1, 1tr into next 3sts, rep from * to end, turn. **Row 2:** ch3, 1tr into next 2 sts, * sk ch, 1tr into next 3sts, rep from * to end, turn. **Row 3:** ch3, 1tr into 1st st, * sk ch, 1tr into next st, work 1sp st into ch2 rows below, 1tr into next st, rep from * to end, turn. **Row 4:** repeat Row 2.

evening sunset

see base design on page 170

variation 2

Cluster stitch Using yarn B, ch5, join with ss to form a ring.
Round 1: work as given for main pattern.
Round 2: ss in between 1st and 2nd sts, ch2, 2tr cl into same sp, ch1, * 3tr in between next 2sts, ch1, rep from * to end working last cluster in between last st and ch2, join with ss into ch2.
Round 3: ss in between 1st and 2nd sts, ch2, 2tr cl into same sp, ch3, * 3tr in between next 2sts, ch3, rep from * to end working last cluster in between last st and ch2, join with ss into ch2. Fasten off yarn B and join in yarn D. **Round 4:** work as per main pattern.

variation 3

Puff stitch Using yarn A, work exactly as per Variation 2, using a puff stitch instead of each 3tr cl.

variation 4

Combination textured sunburst Using yarn C, ch5, join with ss to form a ring. **Round 1:** as per main pattern. **Round 2:** as Round 2 of Variation 3. **Round 3:** as Round 3 of Variation 2. Fasten off yarn C and join in yarn D. **Round 4:** as per main pattern. Fasten off.

variation 5

Popcorn stitch Using yarn E, ch4, join with ss, to form a ring.
Round 1: ch3 (counts as 1tr), 7tr into ring, join with ss into ch3.
Round 2: ch3, * 1 popcorn st into next st, ch3, rep from * to end, join with ss into ch3 behind 1st popcorn. **Round 3:** ss into 1st ch3 sp, ch3, * 1 popcorn st into next ch3 sp, ch3, rep from * to end, join with ss into ch3 behind 1st popcorn. **Round 4:** as per main pattern.

variations

candy

see base design on page 173

variation 2
Block stripes Work as given for main pattern, working increase rows in yarn A and C in a 2-row stripe, then change to yarn D for decrease rows.

variation 3
Block triangles Work as given for main pattern, working all increase rows in yarn D, and then all decrease rows in yarn B.

variation 4
Treble crochet diagonal stripes
Work pattern as given below, changing colours every 2 rows.
Row 1: ch4, 2tr into 4th ch from hook, turn. **Row 2:** ch3, 2tr into 1st st, 1tr into next, 3tr into last st, turn. **Row 3:** ch3, 2tr into 1st st, 1tr into each st until last st, 3tr into last st. Repeat Row 3 until 20sts. **Next row:** ch3, 1tr into each st to end. **Next row (dec):** ch3, sk1, tr2tog, 1tr into to each st until 3 sts, sk1, tr2tog. Repeat last row until 2 sts, tr2 tog. Fasten off.

variation 5
Double treble crochet diagonal stripe Row 1: ch5, 3dtr into 4th ch from hook, turn. **Rows 2–5:** ch4, 2dtr into 1st st, 1dtr into each st to last sts, 3dtr into last st, turn. **Rows 6–10:** ch4, sk1, dtr2tog, 1dtr into each st to last 3sts, sk1, dtr2tog, turn. **Next row:** ch4, ss to ch4 at beg of last row to create a shaped corner. Fasten off.

polka

see base design on page 174

variation 2

Granny polka dot Using yarn D, work as given for main pattern for Rounds 1-3. **Round 4:** Using yarn C, ss into 1st ch sp, ch3 (counts as 1tr), work (1tr, ch3, 2tr) into same sp (1st corner worked), * ch1, sk2, (3tr into next st, ch1, sk2) twice **, work (3tr, ch3, 3tr) into next ch sp, rep from * ending last rep at **, join with ss into ch3. **Round 5:** ss into 1st ch sp, ch3 (counts as 1tr), work (1tr, ch3, 2tr) into same sp (1st corner worked), * ch1, (3tr into next ch sp, ch1) 3 times **, work (3tr, ch3, 3tr) into next ch3 sp, rep from * ending last rep at **, join with ss into ch3.

variation 3

Rounded square Using yarn E, work as given for main pattern for Rounds 1-4. Fasten off yarn C and join in yarn A. **Rounds 5-6:** ss into 1st corner, ch3 (counts as 1tr), work (1dtr, 1tr) into same sp, * work 1htr into each st to next corner, work (1tr, 1dtr, 1tr) into next corner sp, rep from * twice more, then work 1htr into each st to end, join with ss into ch2. Fasten off.

variation 4

Cluster stitch centre Using yarn C, ch4, join with ss to form a ring. **Round 1:** ch3 (counts as 1htr and ch1), * 1htr, ch1, rep from * 10 more times, join with ss into 2nd of ch3. **Round 2:** ss into 1st 1ch sp, ch3 (counts as 1tr), 2tr cl into same sp, ch2, work (3tr cl, ch2) into each ch sp to end, join with ss into ch3. Fasten off yarn C and join in yarn B. **Round 3:** ch1, 1dc into top of 1st cl, * 4 dc into next ch2 sp, 1dc into top of next cl, rep from * ending last rep with 4dc into last ch2 sp, join with ss into ch1. **Round 4:** using yarn F, ch3 (counts as 1tr), 2tr, ch3, 3tr

wedges

see base design on page 177

variation 2

Alternating wedges Using yarn A, ch16. **Rows 1–2:** work as given for main pattern. Fasten off yarn A and join in yarn C. **Row 3:** ch3, * 1tr into 1st st, work (1FPdtr, 1FPtrtr, 1FPquadtr) around same st on prev row, sk3, rep from * ending last rep with 1dc into last st, turn. Keeping pattern correct, change colour at the end of next and every following row. **Row 4:** as Row 2. **Row 5:** ch3, work 1tr into next st, * sk3, (1FPdtr, 1FPtrtr, 1 FPquadtr) around same st on prev row, sk3, rep from * to last 2st, work 1tr into each of last 2sts, turn. **Row 6:** as Row 2. **Row 7:** as Row 3. **Row 8:** as Row 2.

variation 3

Big to small Using yarn C, ch16. **Rows 1–2:** work as for main pattern. **Row 3:** ch3, * sk3, work (1FPquadtr, 1FPtrtr, 1FPdtr) around same st on prev row, 1tr in same st, rep from * to last st, 1tr into last st, turn. Rows 2–3 form the pattern. Repeat to required length, ending on Row 2. Fasten off.

variation 4

Wings Using yarn C, ch20. **Rows 1–2:** work as given for main pattern. Fasten off yarn C and join in yarn B. **Row 3:** ch3, * sk3, work (1FPquadtr, 1FPtrtr, 1FPdtr) around same st on prev row, 1dc in same st, 1dc in next st, (1FPdtr, 1FPtrtr, 1FPquadtr) around next st on prev row, rep from * to last st, 1dc, turn. Fasten off yarn B and join in yarn C. **Row 4:** as Row 2. **Row 5:** as Row 3. **Row 6:** as Row 2.

variation 5

Alternating wings Using yarn C, ch20. **Rows 1–2:** work as for main pattern. Fasten off yarn C and join in yarn A. **Row 3:** ch3, * sk3, work (1FPquadtr, 1FPtrtr, 1FPdtr) around same st on prev row, 1dc in same st, 1dc in next st, work (1FPdtr, 1FPtrtr, 1FPquadtr) around next st on prev row, sk3, rep from * to last st, 1dc, turn. Fasten off yarn A and join in yarn C. **Row 4:** as Row 2. Fasten off yarn C and join in yarn A. **Row 5:** ch3, * 1dc, work (1FPdtr, 1FPtrtr, 1FPquadtr) around same st on row below, sk6, (1FPquadtr, 1FPtrtr, 1FPdtr) around next st on row below, 1dc in top of same st, rep from * to last st, 1dc, turn. **Row 6:** as Row 4.

tweedy square

see base design on page 178

variation 2

Single row stripe Work as given for main pattern, alternating rows between yarn C and yarn D.

variation 4

Half treble crochet Work as given for main pattern using htr throughout and ch3 for turning.

variation 3

Four-row single stripe Work as given for main pattern, using different yarn for each row to create a four-row single stripe pattern.

variation 5

Treble crochet In a yarn colour of your choice, ch27. **Row 1:** 1tr into 4th ch from hook, 1tr into each ch to end, turn (24sts). **Row 2:** ch5, work tr instead of dc into 8th st from hook, * ch2, miss 2, tr into next st, rep from * to end, turn. **Row 3:** ch4, work dtr instead of tr. Rows 2–3 form the pattern; repeat to required length, ending with a row of tr. Fasten off.

variations

knot

see base design on page 181

variation 2
Two-colour knot Work as per Variation 1, but working odd rows in yarn A and even rows in yarn B.

variation 4
Contrast knot Work as per Variation 1 in yarn C, working every dtr in yarn B, carrying yarn C behind as you go.

variation 3
Striped knot Work as per main pattern but Rows 1–2 in yarn C and Rows 3–4 in yarn A, and continue working in striped pattern as set.

variation 5
Dense knot Using A, work as per Variation 1 but leaving out dc rows.

box

see base design on page 182

variation 2

Broken boxes Work as per main pattern, in 1 colour. Do not turn. Using a contrasting colour, work a row of dc in contrasting yarn between each 'box' row, using 3dc for the outer corners for each 'box' and ss into the inner corner. Work dc row with rs facing, then turn to work next 'box' row.

variation 3

Horizontal box stitch Using yarn A, ch20+3 for turning. **Row 1:** 3tr into 4th ch from hook, * sk3, work (1dc, ch3, 3tr) into next st, rep from * to end, working 1dc into last st. **Row 2:** ch3, turn, 3tr into first dc of row below. * 1dc, ch3, 3tr into 3ch, rep from * to end, 1dc into last st, turn. Row 2 forms the pattern. Repeat to required length.

variation 4

Two-colour stripe Work as given for Variation 3, working Row 1 in yarn C and Row 2 in yarn A, and keeping stripe sequence correct. Repeat to required length.

variation 5

Four-colour stripe Work as per Variation 3, working each row in a different coloured stripe, to coordinate with the main pattern.

variations

mary

see base design on page 185

variation 2
Shallow waves
Using yarn D, ch19. **Row 1:** 1dc in 2nd ch from hook, 1dc into each st to end, turn. **Row 2:** ch1, 1dc in each st to end, turn. **Rows 3–5:** ch1, 1dc into next 2sts, (1htr into next st), (1tr into next st) 3 times, (1htr into next st), (1dc into next st) 3 times, rep from * to end, turn. **Rows 6–8:** work as Row 2. **Rows 9–11:** ch1, 1dc into next 6 sts, rep from * to last 4 sts, 1dc into last 4 sts, turn.

variation 3
Shallow sea waves Work as given for Variation 2, using the picture as a guide (using different shades of blue and green).

variation 4
Textured waves
Using yarn A, ch17+3 for turning. **Row 1:** work 1tr into 4th ch from hook, 1tr into each st to end, turn. **Row 2:** ch1, work 1 front-post tr (FPtr) into the st below, work the stitch around the post of the stitch, rather than the top loops, creating a textured effect. * 1tr into next 3sts, 1FPtr into next 3sts. Repeat from * to end, turn. **Row 3:** ch3, 1tr into each st to end, turn. **Row 4:** ch3, 1dtr into 1st st, * 1 FPtr into next 3sts, 1tr into next 3 sts, rep from * once more, 1FPtr into next 3sts, 1tr into last st. **Row 5:** work as Row 3.

variation 5
Caribbean seas Work as Variation 4, working alternate layers in green and aqua yarn for a pretty textured effect.

rainbow

see base design on page 186

variation 2

Two-colour spiral Using yarn A, ch6, join with ss to form a ring. **Round 1:** with yarn A, * ch3, 5tr into ring, rep from * with yarn B.
Round 2: with yarn A, * 2tr into top of ch3, 2tr into each of the next 4sts, rep from * with yarn B.
Round 3: with A, * work (1tr into next st, 2tr into next) 5 times, rep from * with yarn B. **Round 4:** with A, * work (1tr into next st, 2tr into next st) 3 times, 2tr into next st, 1tr into next, 1htr in each of next 3sts, 1dc into each of the next 2sts, ss into next st, ep from * with yarn B.

variation 3

Spiral hexagon Using yarn A, ch6, join with ss to form a ring. **Round 1:** * ch1, 1tr into ring, rep from * with 5 more colours. **Round 2:** * 2tr into each st, rep from * with 5 more colours. **Round 3:** * 1tr into each of the next 3 sts, ch3, sk1 rep from * with 5 more colours. **Round 4:** * 1tr into each of the next 3sts, 2tr into ch3sp, ch3 rep from * with 5 more colours. **Round 5:** * sk1, 1tr into each of the next 4sts, 2tr into ch3 sp, ch4, rep from * with 5 more colours. **Round 6:** * sk1, 1tr into next 5sts, 2tr into ch3 sp, ch4, rep from * with 5 more colours.

variation 4

Spiral flat circle Use yarn F for this variation. **Round 1:** ch2, 2dc, 2htr, 8tr into 2nd ch from hook, keep a firm grip on tail of yarn and pull to close ring. Place stitch marker into the first st of next round. **Round 2:** 2tr into 1st st, 2tr into each st to marker. **Round 3:** 2tr into next st, move marker to 2nd tr, * 1tr into next st, 2tr into next, rep from * to marker. **Round 4:** move marker to 1st st, * 2tr into next st, 1tr into each of the next 2sts, rep from * to marker. **Round 5:** move marker to 1st st, * 2tr into next st, 1tr into each of the next 3sts, taper end by working 1htr into each of the next 2sts, 1dc into next 2sts, ss into next st. Fasten off.

variation 5

Colour-change yarn flat circle Work as per Variation 4, using a self-striping yarn, such as Araucania Chacabuco cotton or Sirdar Escape.

intarsia

see base design on page 189

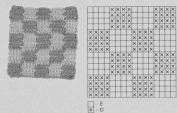

variation 2

Tiny squares Make 3 wrappings of yarns D and E. Using yarn E, ch21. Work from chart, using dc and 1 turning chain, joining in yarns and working colours as shown on the chart.

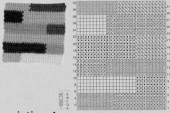

variation 4

Interlocking stripes Using yarn F, ch21. Work from chart, using dc and 1 turning chain, joining in yarns E, B, G and A, working colours as shown on the chart.

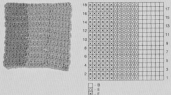

variation 3

Vertical stripes Using yarn B, ch21. Work from chart using dc and 1 turning chain, joining in yarns B and F, working colours as shown on the chart.

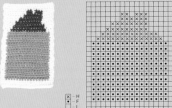

variation 5

House Using yarn I, ch20. Work from chart, using htr and 2 turning chain, joining in yarns F and H, working colours as shown on the chart.

christmas tree

see base design on page 190

variation 2

Tree with tinsel Work as given for main pattern, working tree rows in groups of 3 as follows: 2 rows of yarn C, and 1 row of alternating yarns D, E, F, G and D.

variation 4

Spike stitch Work as given in main pattern, working tree rows in groups of 4 as follows: **Rows 1–2:** work, using yarn C. **Row 3:** * work 1dc into 1st st, work 1 spike stitch into the row below, rep from * to end of tree, complete row as given in chart.

variation 3

Tree with sparkly lights Work as given for main pattern, but work a random contrast colour stitch on each row using yarn A to get the effect of tree lights.

variation 5

Tree motif Using yarn B, ch7. **Row 1:** work 1dc into 2nd ch from hook, 1dc into each st to end, turn. **Rows 2–6:** ch1, 1dc into each st to end, turn. Join in yarn C and ch7. **Row 7:** work 1dc into 2nd ch from hook, work 1ch into each st to end, ch6, turn. **Rows 8–10:** ch1, work 1dc into each st to end. **Rows 11–26:** ch1, sk2, 1dc in each st to end. Fasten off.

variations
baby's blocks

see base design on page 193

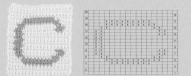

variation 2
Big letter C Make 3 wrappings of yarn A and 2 wrappings of yarn D. Using yarn A, ch19. Work in dc as the chart using the intarsia method and ch1 at the beginning of every row.

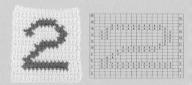

variation 4
Big number 2 Make 3 wrappings of yarn A and 2 wrappings of yarn F. Using yarn A, ch19. Work in dc as the chart shows using the intarsia method and ch1 at the beginning of every row.

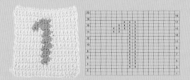

variation 3
Big number 1 Make 3 wrappings of yarn A and 2 wrappings of yarn E. Using yarn A, ch19. Work in dc as the chart shows using the intarsia method and ch1 at the beginning of every row.

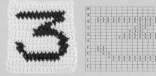

variation 5
Big number 3 Make 3 wrappings of yarn A and 2 wrappings of yarn G. Using yarn A, ch19. Work in dc as the chart shows using the intarsia method and ch1 at the beginning of every row.

shaped motifs

Working with shapes can result in
some unique and lovely projects, such as
a scarf made of octagonal blocks or a baby's
mobile with a dangling sun, moon and stars.
Whatever design you settle on, the colours
and patterns are up to you – and in this
chapter, there is something to suit
everyone's taste.

flat circles

Main pattern: using yarn A, ch5, join into a ring with a ss.

Round 1: ch1, 11dc into ring, join with ss into ch1.

Round 2: ch1, 1dc into 1st st, 2tr into next st, rep from * to end, join with ss into ch1.

Round 3: ch1, * work 2dc into next st, work 1dc into next st, rep from * to to ending last rep at **, join with a ss into the ch1.

Round 4: ch1, * work 2dc into next st, work 1dc into next 2sts, rep from * to ending last rep with 1dc into last st, join with a ss into ch1.

Round 5: ch1, * work 2dc into next st, work 1dc into next 3sts, rep from * to ending last rep with 1dc into last 2sts, join with a ss into ch1.

Round 6: ch1, * work 2dc into next st, work 1dc into next 4sts, rep from * to ending last rep with 1dc into last 3sts, join with a ss into ch1.

Round 7: ch1, * work 2dc into next st, work 1dc into next 5 sts, rep from * to ending last rep with 1dc into last 4sts, join with a ss into ch1. Fasten off, weave in ends.

Project notes: Cushion cover.
Work 2 pieces in single row colour stripes as per Variation 4 to match the size of the cushion pad. Sew the circles halfway together, insert the pad and sew around the rest of the outer edge.

materials

■ 4mm hook
■ King Cole Bamboo Cotton in Rose (A), Opal (B), Plum (C)

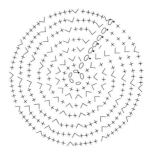

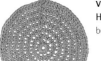

variation 1

see other variations on page 258

Half treble crochet Using yarn A, work as given for main pattern, using htr and ch2 at beginning of each round throughout.

granny circles

Main pattern: using yarn A, ch4, join with ss to form a ring.

Round 1: ch3 (counts as 1tr), 1tr into ring, * ch1, 2tr into ring, rep from * 4 more times, ch1, join with ss into top of ch3.

Round 2: ss into 1st st and ch1sp, ch3 (counts as 1tr), 1tr, ch1, 2tr into same space, ch1, * work (2tr, ch1, 2tr) into next ch1sp, ch1, rep from * 4 more times, join with ss into top of ch3.

Round 3: ss into 1st set of sts and ch1sp, ch3 (counts as 1tr), 2tr into same sp, ch1, * 3tr into next ch1sp, ch, rep from * to end, join with ss into top of ch3.

Round 4: work as Round 3.

Round 5: ss into 1st st and ch1sp, ch3 (counts as 1tr), 1tr, ch1, 2tr into same space, ch1, * (2tr into next ch1sp, ch1) twice **, work (2tr,

ch1, 2tr) into next ch1 sp, ch1, rep from * 3 more times ending last rep at **, join with ss into ch3.

Rounds 6–7: work as Round 3.

Round 8: ss into 1st st and ch1sp, ch3 (counts as 1 tr), 1tr, ch1, 2tr into same space, ch1, * (2tr into next ch1sp, ch1) 3 more times **, work (2tr, ch1, 2tr) into next ch1sp, ch1, rep from * 3 more times ending last rep at **, join with ss into ch3.

Rounds 9–10: work as Round 3. Fasten off.

Project notes: Stool cover. Make as many rounds as needed to fit the diameter of your stool, then work rounds of dc with NO increases to make the snug sides for the cover. To ensure it fits the stool top, work several rounds of decreasing dc (sk1, dc into next st) to give it a

materials

- 4mm hook
- Sublime Baby Cashmere Merino Silk DK in Vanilla (A), Caterpillar (B), Splash (C), Teddy Red (D), Pansy (E)

stretchy edge to fit underneath the stool top.

see other variations on page 259

variation 1

Coaster Add a shell edge to turn the granny circle into a mat or a coaster. Join yarn B into any st on the outer edge and work as follows: **Round 1:** ch1, 5tr into 1st ch1 sp, ch1, * 1dc into next ch1sp, ch1, 5tr into next ch1sp, rep from * to end.

twinkle

Main pattern: using yarn A, ch4, join with ss to form a ring.

Round 1: ch3 (counts as 1tr), 9tr into the ring, join with ss into ch3.

Round 2: * ch5, 1dc into 2nd ch from hook, work into rem 3ch as follows, 1htr into next ch, 1tr into next ch, 1tr into last ch, sk1, ss into next st, repeat from * to end, join with ss into base of ch5. Fasten off.

materials

- 4mm hook
- Sublime extra fine merino wool DK in Roasted Pepper (A), Pistachio (B): Ver 1, 2, 4
- Colinette Cadenza in Sweet Dreams (C): Ver 3, 5

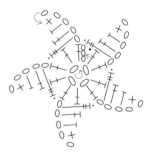

variation 1

see other variations on page 260

Work as given for main pattern, Round 1 in yarn A and Round 2 in yarn B.

solar

Notes: do not work into turning chain for the rounds.

Main pattern: using yarn A, ch6, join with ss to form a ring.

Round 1: ch1, 10dc into ring, join with ss into trc.

Round 2: ch1, 2dc in each st to end, join with ss into trc.

Round 3: ch1, * 1dc into each of the next 3sts, 2dc in next st rep from * to end, join with ss into trc.

Round 4: ch1, * 1dc into each of the next 4sts, 2dc in next st rep from * to end, join with ss into trc.

Work each point as follows, counting ch3 as stitch.

Row 1: ch1, 1dc into next 6 sts, turn. Work into ch1 and 6sts only.

Row 2: ch1, 1dc in each st across, turn.

Row 3: ch1, dc2 tog, 1dc into each of the next 4sts, dc2tog, turn.

Row 4: work as Row 2. Do not work into tch.

Row 5: ch1, dc2tog, 1dc into each of the next sts, dc2tog, turn.

Row 6: work as Row 2. Do not work into tch.

Row 7: ch1 (dc2tog) twice. Fasten off yarn.

Rejoin yarn to main circle and work a further 4 points. Fasten off.

materials

- 4mm hook: main, Var 2–5
- King Cole Bamboo Cotton in Yellow (A), Cobalt (B), Plum (C), Moss (D), Rose (E), Cream (F)
- 6mm hook: Ver 1
- Sublime Chunky Merino Tweed in Forage (G), Glover (H)

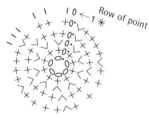

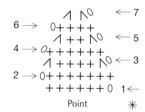

variation 1

see other variations on page 261

Alternate colours Work as given for main pattern with Round 1 in yarn G and Round 2 in yarn H. Keeping pattern correct, work in stripe sequence as set for rounds and rows.

galaxy

Main pattern: using yarn F, ch5, join with ss to form a ring.

Round 1: ch3 (counts as first tr), 2tr into ring, * ch3, 3tr into ring, rep from * 3 more times, ch3, join with ss into ch3.

Round 2: ss along and into 1st ch3sp, ch3 (counts as 1tr), 2tr, ch3, 3tr same sp (1st corner worked), ch1, * work (3tr, ch3, 3tr) into next ch3sp, ch1, rep from * to end, join with ss into ch3.

Round 3: ss along and into next corner sp, ch3 (counts as 1tr), 2tr, ch4, 3tr into same sp (1st point worked), 1dc into next ch1sp, * work (3tr, ch4, 3tr) into next ch3sp, 1dc into next ch1sp, rep from * to end, join with ss into ch3. Fasten off.

Project notes: Garland. String stars together to make a festive garland.

materials

- 5mm hook: Var 1–4
- Rowan All Seasons Cotton in Damson (A), Blush (B), Jacuzzi (C), String (D), Hedge (E)
- 4mm hook: main
- Debbie Bliss Cotton DK (F)

....

see other variations on page 262

variation 1

Twinkly granny star Using yarn A, work as given for main pattern for Rounds 1–3. Change to yarn B and work edging as follows: **Round 4:** ch1, 1dc into 1st 2sts, work (1dc, MP – ch3, 1ss into 3rd ch from hook, 1dc) into 1st ch4sp, * 1dc into next 7sts, (1dc, MP, 1dc) into next ch4sp, rep from * to ending last rep with 1dc into last st, join with ss into ch1.

flora

Main pattern: using yarn A, ch3, join with ss to form a ring.

Round 1: ch1 (counts as 1dc), 9dc into a ring, join with ss into ch1.

Round 2: * ch2, work (1htr, 1tr, 1tr, 1tr, 1htr) into next st, ch2, 1dc into next st, rep from * 4 more times. Fasten off yarn.

materials

- 4mm hook
- Debbie Bliss Cotton DK in Green (A), Red (B), Blue (C), Pigeon (D), Damson (E)

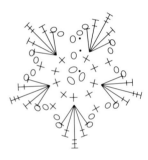

see other variations on page 263

variation 1
Two-colour flower Work as given for main pattern, working Round 1 in yarn A and Round 2 in yarn B.

in bloom

Main pattern: using yarn A, ch3 and join with ss to form a ring.

Round 1: ch3 (counts as 1tr), 9tr into ring, join with ss into ch3.

Round 2: ch3 (counts as 1tr), 1tr into same st, 2tr in each st to end, join with ss, into ch3.

Round 3: ch3 (counts as 1tr), 1tr into same st, * 1tr into next st, 2sts into next st, rep from * to end, join with ss into ch3.

Round 4: same as Round 2.

Round 5: * sk2, 5tr into next st, sk2, ss to next st (1st petal worked), rep from * to end, working last rep

with ss into 1st of 5tr at beg of round. Fasten off.

Project notes: Coasters. Make up 6 of the main pattern for a set.

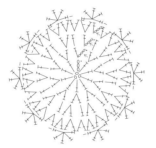

materials

- 4mm hook: main, Var 2, 3, 5
- King Cole Bamboo Cotton DK in Oyster (A), Yellow (B), Plum (C), Opal (D), Aqua (E), Red (F), White (H), Moss (J)
- 5mm hook: Var 4
- Rowan Cotton Glace in Persimmon (I)
- Debbie Bliss Cotton DK in Brown (G)

---

see other variations on page 264

variation 1
Two-colour flower with 13 petals Using yarn F, ch3, join with ss to form a ring. **Rounds 1–2:** work as given for main pattern. **Round 3:** as Round 2 of main pattern. Break off yarn F and join in yarn J. **Round 4:** ch1 (counts as 1st sc), 1sc into each st to end, join with ss into ch1. **Round 5:** * ch1, work (1htr, 1tr) into next st and (1tr, 1htr) into next st, ch1, ss into next st, rep from * to ending last rep with ss into base of ch1. Fasten off.

posy

Main pattern: using yarn A, ch4 and join with ss to form a ring.

Round 1: ch3 (counts as 1tr), 11tr into ring, join with ss into ch3.

Round 2: ch1, 3tr into next st (1st petal worked), ch1, ss into next st, rep from * to end, ss into ch1.

Work next round at the back of work to create 6 loops.

Round 3: ch3, sk petal, 1dc into back of ss, rep from * to end, join with ss into ch3.

Round 4: ch1, 5tr into 1st ch3 loop, ch1, dc into next st, * 5tr into next ch3 loop, 1dc into next st, rep from * to end, join with ss into ch1.

Project notes: Flower brooch. Attach a brooch to the back of the posy. Sew a button to the centre front of the posy.

materials

- 5mm hook
- Rowan All Seasons Cotton in 242 Blush (A), 241 Plum (B), 246 Hedge (C), 239 Jacuzzi (D)
- button: main project

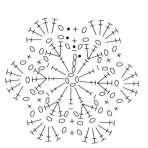

see other variations on page 265

variation 1

Two-tone flower Work as given for main pattern working Rounds 1–3 in yarn A and Round 4 in yarn B.

fall in love

Main pattern: using yarn A, ch10.

Round 1: 1tr into 3rd ch from hook, work (1tr, 1htr, 1dtr, 1tr, 1htr, 1dc, 1dc) along ch, make picot as follows: (ch3, ss into 1st ch), then work back along the underside of chain as follows: (1dc, 1dc, 1htr, 1tr, 1dtr, 1htr, 1tr). Fasten off, leaving a short tail for stalk.

materials

- 3mm hook: Var 2, 3, 4, 5
- Rowan Cotton Glace in Persimmon (D), Ochre (C), Dijon (B)
- 4mm hook: main, Var 1
- Debbie Bliss Cotton DK in 015 Brown (A)

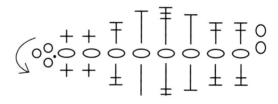

see other variations on page 266

variation 1

Picot edge leaf Using yarn A, work as given for main leaf, do not fasten off yarn at the end of Round 1, work picot edge as follows: **Round 2:** make 1st picot (MP), ch3, ss into 1st ch, sk1, ss into next st, * MP, sk1, ss into next st, rep from * to end, ch4 for stalk. Fasten off.

rectangles

Main pattern: ch30+1 for turning.

Row 1: sk1,1dc in each ch to end, working last dc into top of turning ch.

Rows 2–4: repeat Row 1. Fasten off.

Project notes: 'Paper' chain with main block. Make up 12 rectangles then sew up the ends with mattress stitch, interlocking the rectangles as you go. Increase the number of rectangles for a longer chain.

materials

- 4mm hook
- Debbie Bliss Cotton DK in 15 Red (A), 43 Green (B), 32 Brown (C), 19 Grey (D), 09 Pale Blue (E)

see other variations on page 267

variation 1

Two-colour rectangles Work as given for main pattern. Using yarn B, work a row of contrasting dc all around the edge. Join in yarn A, ch1, then work 1 dc into every st, 3dc into the corner sts. Join with ss. Fasten off.

diamonds are forever

Main pattern: using yarn F, ch2.

Row 1: 2dc into 2nd ch from hook, turn.

Row 2: ch1 (turning chain), 1dc into first st, 2dc into 2nd st, turn.

Row 3: ch1 (turning chain), 1dc into 1st st, 1dc into 2nd st, 2dc into last st, turn.

Rows 4–15 (inc): ch1 (counts as 1 dc), 1dc into 1st st, work 1dc into each st, 2dc into last st, turn. **Rows 16–30 (dec):** sk1, 1dc into next st, 1dc into each st to end turn. Fasten off.

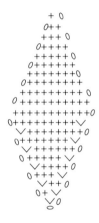

materials

■ 4mm hook
■ Debbie Bliss Rialto in Duck Egg (A), Gold (B), Earth (C), Emerald (D), Apple (E), Scarlet (F)

see other variations on page 268

variation 1
Half treble crochet diamond Using yarn A, ch3. **Row 1:** 2htr into 3rd ch from hook, turn. Work as given for main pattern, working htr throughout and ch2 for turning. Fasten off.

octagons

Main pattern: using a 12mm hook and yarn I, ch5, join with ss to form a ring.

Round 1: ch3 (counts as 1tr), work 15tr in ring, join with ss into ch3.

Round 2: using yarn J, ch3 (counts as 1tr), 2tr into same st, 1tr in next st, * 3tr in next st, 1tr in next st, rep from * to end, join with ss into ch3.

Round 3: using yarn K, ch3 (counts as 1tr), 2tr into same st, 1tr into next 3sts, * 3tr into next st, 1tr into next 3sts, rep from * to end, join with ss into ch3.

Round 4: using yarn I, ch3 (counts as 1tr), 2tr into same st, 1tr into next 5sts, * 3tr into next st, 1tr into next 5sts, rep from * to end, join with ss into ch3. Fasten off yarn I, join in yarn J.

Round 5: ch3 (counts as 1tr), 2tr into same st, 1tr into next 7sts, * 3tr into next st, 1tr into next 7sts, rep from * to end, join with ss into ch3. Fasten off yarn J and join in yarn K.

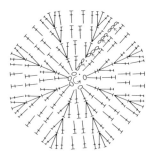

materials

- 4mm hook: Var 1–4
- Sublime Baby Cashmere Merino DK in Piglet (A), Puffin (B), Little Miss Plum (C), Caterpillar (D), White (H)
- 12mm hook: main
- hoopla yarn blue (I), pink (J), cream (K)

Round 6: ch3 (counts as 1tr), 2tr into same st, 1tr into next 9sts, * 3tr into next st, 1tr into next 9sts, rep from * to end, join with ss into ch3. Fasten off.

see other variations on page 269

variation 1

Half treble crochet Using yarn C, ch5, join with ss to form a ring. Work as given for main pattern using htr throughout and ch2 for turning. Fasten off.

henry

Main pattern: using yarn A, ch4, join with ss to form a ring.

Round 1: ch1 (counts as 1tr), 11dc into a ring, join with a ss into the ch1.

Round 2: ch1 (counts as 1tr), * 3dc into next st, 1dc into next st, rep from * 4 more times, 3dc into last st, join with a ss in to ch1.

Round 3: ch1 (counts as 1tr), 1dc into next st, * 3dc into next st, 1dc into each of the next 3sts, rep from * 4 more times, 3dc into next st, 1dc into last st, join with a ss in to ch1.

Round 4: ch1 (counts as 1tr), 1dc into each of next 2st, * 3dc into next st, 1dc into each of next 5sts, rep from * 4 more times, 3dc into next st, 1dc into each of the next 2sts, join with a ss in to ch1. Fasten off.

Project notes: Dcarf. Make 10 blocks, in each of the 5 colours., totalling 50 blocks. Using a darning needle, sew the blocks together to make a scarf.

materials

■ 4mm hook
■ King Cole Bamboo Cotton in Plum (A), Cobalt (B), Moss (C), Damson (D), Opal (E)

see other variations on page 270

variation 1

Alternate stripes Work as given for main pattern, working in htr throughout and ch2 for turning chain. Work Rounds 1 and 3 in yarn A. Work Rounds 2 and 4 in yarn C. Fasten off.

meadow hexagons

Main pattern: using yarn F, ch4, join with ss to form a ring.

Round 1: ch1 (counts as 1tr), 11dc into ring, join with ss into tch.

Round 2: ch1, 3tr into 1st st, * ch1, ss into next st, ch1, 3tr into next st, rep from * 5 more times to make 6 petals, join with ss into back loop of ch1.

Work next round at the back of work to create 6 loops. Work next round to the back of work.

Round 3: * ch2, miss 1st petal, ss into back of next ss, rep from * to end, join with ss into 1st ch at beg of round. Break off yarn F and join in yarn B.

Round 4: ch3 (counts as 1tr), 2tr into 1st ch2 loop, * ch3, 3tr into next ch2 loop, rep from * to end, join with ss to top of ch3.

Round 5: ss into next 2sts and 1st ch2 sp, ch3 (counts as 1tr), 1tr, ch2, 2tr into same sp, ch1, * work (2tr, ch2, 2tr) into next ch2 sp, ch1, rep from * to end, join with ss in to ch3.

Round 6: ss into next st and 1st ch2 sp, ch3 (counts as 1tr), 1tr, ch2, 2tr into same sp, ch1, 3tr into next ch sp, * work (2tr, ch2, 2tr) into next ch2sp, ch1, 3tr into next ch sp, rep from * to end, join with ss in to ch3.

Round 7: ss into next st and 1st ch2 sp, ch3 (counts as 1tr), 1tr, ch2, 2tr into same sp, (3tr into next ch sp) twice, * work (2tr, ch2, 2tr) into next ch2sp, (3tr into next ch sp) twice, rep from * to end, join with ss in to ch3.

materials

- 4mm hook
- King Cole Bamboo Cotton DK in Moss (A), Aqua (B), Yellow (C), Rose Pink (D),

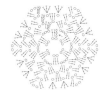

see other variations on page 272

variation 1

Solid hexagon edge Using yarn B, work Rounds 1–4 as given for main pattern. Break off yarn B and join in yarn F. **Round 5:** ch3 (counts as 1tr), 1tr into next 2sts, * work (2tr, ch3, 2tr) into next ch3 sp, sk1, 1tr into next 2sts, rep from * 4 times, work (2tr, ch3, 1tr) into last ch3 sp, join with ss into ch3. **Round 6:** ch3 (counts as 1tr), 1tr into next 3 sts, * work (2tr, ch3, 2tr) into next ch3 sp, sk1, 1tr into next 5sts, rep from * 4 times, work (2tr, ch3, 2tr) into last ch3sp, 1tr into last st, join with ss into ch3.

cheep cheep

Main pattern: using yarn A, ch4.

Row 1: 1dc in 2nd ch from hook and each st to end dc.

Row 2: ch1, 2dc into 1st st, 1dc in next st, 2dc in last st, turn.

Row 3: ch1, 2dc into 1st st, 1dc in next 3sts, 2dc in last st, turn.

Row 4: ch1, 1dc into 1st 3sts, 2dc into next st, 1dc into last 3sts, turn.

Row 5: ch1, 1dc into 1st st, 2dc into next st, 1dc into next 4sts, 2dc into next st, 1dc into last st, turn.

Row 6: 1dc into 1st st, 2dc into next st, 1dc into next 6sts, 2dc into next st, 1dc into last st, turn.

Rows 7–8: ch1, 1dc into each st to end, turn.

Row 9: ch1, 1dc into 1st st, dc2tog over next 2sts, 1dc into next 6sts, dc2tog over next 2sts, 1dc into last st, turn.

Row 10: ch1, 1dc into 1st st, dc2tog over next 2sts, 1dc into next 4sts, dc2tog over next 2sts, 1dc into last st, turn.

Row 11: work as Row 7.

Row 12: ch1, 1dc into 1st st, dc2tog over next 2sts, 1dc into next 2sts, dc2tog over next 2sts, 1dc into last st, turn.

Row 13: work as Row 7.

Row 14: ch1, 1dc into 1st st, sk1, dc2tog over next 2sts, sk1, 1dc into last st. Fasten off.

materials

- 4mm hook
- Sublime Baby Cashmere Merino DK in Puffin (A), Puzzle (B), Piglet (C), Teddy Red (D)

see other variations on page 273

variation 1

Striped Work as given for main pattern and as follows: Rows 1–4 in yarn A, Rows 5–6 in yarn B, Rows 7–8 in yarn A, Rows 9–10 in yarn B and Rows 11–14 in yarn A. Fasten off.

beachcombing

Main pattern: Using yarn A, ch4, join with ss to form a ring.

Round 1: ch1 (counts as 1st dc), 13dc into ring, do not join. Place stitch marker into the first st of the round.

Round 2: 2dc into each st, to end. Move the stitch marker to 1st st of next and every following round.

Round 3: * 1dc next 2sts, 2dc into the next st, rep from * to end.

Round 4: * 1dc next 3sts, 2dc into the next st, rep from * to end.

Round 5: * 1dc next 4 sts, 2dc into the next st, rep from * to end.

Round 6: * 1dc next 5sts, 2dc into the next st, rep from * to end.

materials

- 6mm hook: main, Var 1–4
- Drops Karisma in Rust (A), Green (B), Sublime Chunky Merino Tweed in Forage (C)
- 4mm hook
- King Cole Smooth in Pewter (D), Spearmint (E), Cobalt (F), Rose (G)
- 10mm hook: Var 5
- hoopla yarn

see other variations on page 274

variation 1
Work as given for main pattern, working Rounds 1, 3 and 5 in yarn A and Rounds 2 and 4 in yarn B.

flutterby

Main pattern: using yarn B, ch4, join with ss to form a ring.

Round 1: ch4, 3tr into ring, ch3, ss into ring, ch3, 3tr into ring, ch4, ss into ring,* ch3, 3tr into ring, ch3, ss into ring, rep from * once more. Fasten off.

Using the picture as a guide, make the abdomen and antennae parts by sewing around the middle with yarn A.

materials

- 4mm hook
- King Cold Bamboo Cotton in Moss (A), Rose (B), Cobalt (C), Aqua (D), Plum (E), Purple (F), Yellow (G)

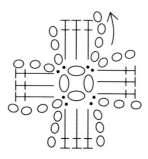

see other variations on page 275

variation 1

High flying Using yarn C, ch4, join with ss to form a ring. **Round 1:** * ch2, 3tr into ring, ch2, ss into ring, rep from * 3 more times. Fasten off and finish as in main pattern.

bunting

Main pattern: using yarn A, ch15+2 for turning. Turn.

Row 1: 1htr into 3rd ch from hook, 1htr into each ch to end, turn.

Row 2: ch2, sk1, 1htr into each st to 2sts, htr2tog, turn.

Row 3: ch2, 1htr into each st to end, turn.

Rows 2–3 form decrease pattern; repeat these rows until 5sts remain.

Next row: ch2, htr2tog, 1htr, hd2tog, turn.

Next row: ch2, htr3tog. Fasten off.

Project notes: Bunting. Make up 2 triangles in each colour for bunting. Make a chain of 20, then dc along the top of the triangles, with 10ch between each triangle.

materials

- 4mm hook
- Debbie Bliss Cotton DK in Plum (A), Teal (B), Hot Pink (C), Apple Green (D), Mushroom (E)

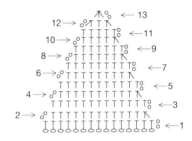

see other variations on page 276

variation 1

Work triangle as main pattern. Join in yarn B to right hand top corner of triangle, work picot edge as follows: ch1, 1dc into 1st st, * sk1, ch3, 1dc into next st, rep from * to end. Fasten off.

stella

Main pattern: using yarn A, ch4, join with ss to form a ring.

Round 1: ch3 (counts as 1st tr), 2tr into ring, * ch3, 3tr into ring, rep from * once more, ch3, join with ss into top of ch3.

Round 2: ss along and into to first ch3sp. Ch3 (counts as 1st tr) work (2tr, 4ch, 3tr) into first ch sp,* ch3, (3tr, 4ch, 3tr) into next ch3sp, rep from * once more, 3ch, join with ss into top of ch3.

Round 3: ss along and into to 1st ch3sp, ch3 (counts as 1st tr) work (2tr, 4ch, 3tr) into same sp, * 3ch, 3tr into next ch3sp, 3ch, (3tr, 4ch, 3tr) into next ch3sp, rep from * once more, 3ch, join with ss into top of ch3. Fasten off.

materials

■ 4mm hook
■ Sublime Baby Cashmere Merino Silk DK in Seesaw (A), Vanilla (B), Teddy Red (C)

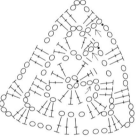

see other variations on page 277

variation 1

Tri-colour triangle Using yarn A, ch4, join with ss to form a ring. Work as given for main pattern with Round 1 in yarn A, Round 2 in yarn B and Round 3 in yarn C. Fasten off.

big love

Main pattern: using yarn A, ch3, join with ss to form a ring.

Round 1: ch3 (counts as 1tr), 2tr into ring, * ch3, 3tr into ring, rep from * twice more, ch3, join with ss into ch3.

Round 2: ss along and into 1st ch3sp, ch3 (counts as 1tr), 2tr ch3, 3tr into same sp ch3, work * 3tr, ch3, 3tr into next ch3sp, ch3, rep * twice more, join with ss in to ch3.

Round 3: ss along and into 1st ch3sp, ch1, 1dc into same sp, 7dtr into next ch3sp, ch4, ss into each st and ch up to last set of 3tr, ch4, 7dtr into last ch3sp, join with ss into 1dc. Fasten off.

materials

- 4mm hook
- Debbie Bliss Cotton DK in Pale Blue (A), Teal (B), Red (C), Purple (D), Mustard (E)

see other variations on page 278

variation 1

Solid granny square centre Using yarn B, work Round 1 as given for main pattern.
Round 2: ch3 (counts as 1tr), 1tr, ch2, 2tr into corner ch3sp, * 1tr into next 3sts, work (2tr, ch2, 2tr) into next corner ch3sp, rep from * twice more, 1tr into next 3sts, join with ss into ch3. **Round 3:** work as per main pattern.

kind hearts

Main pattern: using yarn A, ch3, join with ss to form a ring.

Round 1: ch3 (counts as 1tr), 11tr into ring, join with ss into ch3.

Round 2: ch1, sk ch3 of prev round, 1dc into next st, work (1htr, 1tr, 1htr) into next st, 1dc into next 3sts, ch1, 1tr into next st, ch1, 1dc into next 3sts, work (1tr, 1htr, 1tr) into next st, 1dc into last st, ss into ch3.

Round 3: ch1, 1dc into next 2sts, 3dc into next st, 1dc into nest 4sts, 2dc into next chsp, 3dc into next st, 2dc into next ch sp, 1dc into next 4sts, 3dc into next st, 1dc into last 2sts, ch1, ss into ch1.

Project notes: Heart garland.
Work 3 hearts in each colour, join using ch in contrasting colour, 15 ch between each heart, and ss to top of each heart to join.

materials

- 4mm hook
- Debbie Bliss Cotton DK in Red (A), Pale Green (B), Mushroom (C), Pale Blue (D)

see other variations on page 279

variation 1

Work Rounds 1–2 as given for main pattern in yarn A, and Round 3 in yarn B.

pot holder

Main pattern: using yarn A, ch6, join with ss to form a ring.

Round1: ch3 (counts as 1tr), 11tr into the ring, join with ss in to ch3.

Round 2: ch3 (counts as 1tr), 1tr into 1st st, * 2tr next st, rep from * to end, join with ss in to ch3.

Round 3: ch3 (counts as 1tr), 1tr into 1st st, * 1tr into next st, 2tr next st, rep from* to end, join with ss in to ch3.

Round 4: ch4 (counts as 1tr and ch1), 1tr into 1st st, * sk2, work (1tr, ch1, 1tr) into next st, rep from* to end, join with ss in to ch3.

Round 5: ch3 (counts as 1tr), 1tr, ch1, 2tr into 1st ch1sp, * sk2, work (2tr, ch1 2tr) into next ch1sp, rep from * to end, join with ss into ch3.

Round 6: work as Round 5.

Round 7: ch3 (counts as 1tr), 2tr into 1st ch1sp, ch1, 3tr into same sp, work (3tr, ch1, 3tr) next ch2 sp, ch1 rep from * to end, join with ss into ch3.

Round 8: work as Round 7.

Round 9: ss into 1st ch2sp, ch3, 7tr into same sp, * 8tr into next ch1 sp, rep from * to end. Break of yarn A and join in yarn B.

Round 10: ch1, * 1dc across 7sts, then work 1dc, ch1 into next and every foll gap down towards the centre of the flower and back up to the next petal, rep from * starting next rep with 1dc across 8sts.

see other variations on page 280

variation 1

Square pot holder Work as pattern below in stripe sequence as follow. Round 1: J. Round 2: K. Round 3: L. Round 4: J. Round 5: M. Rounds 6-7: J. Then ch 5, join with ss to form ring. **Round 1:** ch3, 15tr into ring, join with a ss into ch3. **Round 2:** ch3, 4tr into base of ch, 1tr into next 3sts, * 5tr into next st,1tr into next 3sts, rep from * to end, join with ss into ch3. **Round 3:** ch3, 1tr into next st, * 5tr into next st, 1tr into next 7sts, rep from * ending last rep with 1tr into last 5sts, join with ss into ch3. **Round 4:** ch3, 1tr into next 2sts, work (2tr, ch2, 2tr) into next st, 1tr into next 11sts, rep from * ending last rep with 1tr into last 7sts, join with ss into ch3. **Round 5:** ch3, 1tr into next 4sts, work (2tr, ch2, 2tr) into next ch2sp, 1tr into next 15sts, rep from * ending last rep with 1tr into last 9sts, join with ss into ch3. **Round 6:** ch3, 1tr into next 6sts, work (2tr, ch2, 2tr) into next ch2sp, 1tr into next 19sts, rep from* ending last rep with 1tr into last 11sts, join with ss into ch3. **Round 7:** ch1, 1dc into next 8sts, work 5dc into next ch2sp, 1tr into next 23sts, rep from* ending last rep with 1tr into last 11sts. Make loop as follows, work 10ch, ss into top of ch3, turn and work 13dc into loop, join with ss into outer edge of square.

materials

- 4mm hook
- Patons double knit cotton in Purple (A), Lilac (B), Foxglove (C), Raffia (D), Denim (E), Maroon (F), White (G), Lilac (H), Nougat (I)
- Rowan Kid Classic DK in Victoria (J), Cherry Red (K), Tea Rose (L), Crushed Velvet (M)
- King Cole Bamboo Cotton DK in Moss (N), Rose (O), Damson (P)
- Sirdar Supersoft Aran in White (Q), Light Teal (R)

blizzard

Main pattern: using yarn A, ch6, join with ss to form a ring.

Round 1: ch3 (counts as 1tr), 15tr in to ring, join with ss into ch3.

Round 2: ch5 (counts as 1tr and ch2), 1tr in base of 5ch, sk1, * work (1tr, ch2, 1tr) into next st, sk1, rep from * 6 more times, join with a ss into top of ch3.

Round 3: ss into 1st ch2sp, ch3 (counts as 1tr), 1tr, ch3, 2tr in same sp, * work (2tr, ch3, 2tr) into next ch2 sp, rep from * 6 more times, join with a ss into top of ch3.

Round 4: ss into next 2sts and 1st ch2 sp, * make picot (MP) as follows: (ch3, ss into 3rd ch from hook) 3 times, work 1dc into next 4sts, rep from * 7 times, ending last rep working 1dc into last 2sts.

Make loop by working ch10, ss into next st. Fasten off.

Project notes: Christmas tree ornament. Before fastening off yarn, chain 10 and ss to block to make a chain. Loop to hang on the tree or as part of a garland.

materials

■ 4mm hook
■ Sublime Baby Cashmere Merino Silk DK in Vanilla (A), DMC Lumina in Silver (B)

see other variations on page 282

variation 1

Sparkling snowflake Work as given for main pattern in yarn B for a sparkly effect.

cute crochet

Main pattern: to make a rainbow, using violet yarn, ch8.

Row 1: 1dc into 2nd ch from hook, 1tr into next ch, 2tr into next ch, 1tr into next ch, 2tr into next ch, 1tr into next ch, 1dc into last ch, turn. Break off violet and join in indigo.

Row 2: ch1, 1dc into next 2sts, 2dc into next st, 1dc into next 3 sts, 2dc into next st, 1dc into each st to end, turn. Break off indigo and join in blue.

Row 3: ch1, 1dc into 1st 2sts, * 2dc into next st, 1dc into next 2 sts, rep from * to end, turn. Break off blue and join in green.

Row 4: work as Row 3. Break off green and join in yellow.

Row 5: ch1, 1dc into 1st 2sts, 2dc into next st, 1dc into next 3sts, 2dc into next st, 1dc into next 4sts, 2dc into next st, 1dc into next 3sts, 2dc into next st, 1dc into each st to end, turn. Break off yellow and join in orange.

Row 6: ch1, 1dc into 1st 2sts, 2dc into next st, 1dc into next 4sts, 2dc into next st, 1dc into next 6sts, 2dc into next st, 1dc into next 4sts, 2dc into next st, 1dc into each st to end, turn. Break off orange.

Row 7: ch1, 1dc into next 12sts, 2dc into each of the next 2 sts, 1dc into each st to end. Fasten off.

Project notes: Key chain or mobile. Using black embroidery

materials

- 3mm hook
- Any DK weight yarn in a rainbow spectrum of colours

silk, stitch a face onto each block or attach to a key chain for a key ring. Alternatively, use all the emblems together to make a baby's mobile.

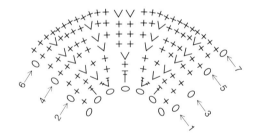

see other variations on page 283

variation 1

Crescent moon Using yellow yarn, ch12. **Row 1:** 1dc in 2nd ch from hook, 1dc into next ch, 2tr in next ch7, 1dc into each ch to end, turn. **Row 2:** sk1 * dc in next 2sts, 2dc into next ch, rep from * to end, ss into last st. Fasten off.

variations

flat circles

see base design on page 211

variation 2
Treble crochet Using yarn B, work as given for main pattern, using tr and ch 3 at beg of each round throughout.

variation 3
Double treble crochet Using yarn C, work as given for main pattern, using dtr and ch 4 at beg of each round throughout.

variation 4
Stripe Work as given for Variation 2 working single round stripe sequence, work Round 1 in yarn A, Round 2 in yarn B, Round 3 in yarn C, repeat stripe to end.

variation 5
Multi stitch In yarn B, work Rounds 1–2 as given for Variation 1. Work Rounds 3–4 as given for Variation 2 in yarn C and join in yarn A. **Round 5:** ch4, * 2dtr into next st, rep from * to end, ss into top of ch4. **Round 6:** ch4, * dtr into next st, 1dtr into next 2sts, rep from * to end, ss into top of ch4.

granny circles

see base design on page 212

variation 2

Cluster stitch Using yarn C, ch4, join with ss to form ring. **Round 1:** ch3 (counts as 1dc), 2tr cl into ring, ch1, * 3tr cl into ring, ch1, rep from * 4 more times, join with ss into top of 1st cluster. **Round 2:** ss into 1st ch1sp, ch2, 1tr (counts as 1st cluster), ch1, 2tr cl into same sp, ch1, * work (2tr cl, ch1, 2tr cl) into next ch1sp, ch1, rep from * to end, join with ss into top of 1st cluster. **Round 3:** ss into 1st ch1sp, ch2, 1tr 2cl into same sp, ch2, * 3tr cl into next ch1sp, ch1, rep from * to end, join with ss into top of 1st cluster. **Round 4:** ss into 1st ch1sp, ch2, 1tr (counts as 1st cluster), ch2, 2tr cl into same sp, ch2, * work (2tr cl, ch2, 2tr cl) into next ch1sp, ch2, rep from * to end, join with ss into top of 1st cluster.

variation 4

Popcorn stitch Using yarn E work as given for Variation 3 working a popcorn stitch instead of puff stitch throughout.

variation 5

Combination stitches Using yarn A, ch4, join with ss to form ring. Change colours as required using yarns B, C, D. **Round 1:** work as main pattern. **Round 2:** work as Variation 2. **Round 3:** work as Variation 3. **Round 4:** work as main pattern. **Round 5:** work as Round 4 of Variation 4. **Round 6:** work as Round 3 of main pattern. **Round 7:** work as Variation 1, working ch1,5 dc, ch1 into next ch1sp, sc into next throughout.

variation 3

Puff stitch Using yarn D, ch4, join with ss to form ring. Work each round as given for main pattern with the changes below.
Round 1: work 1PS instead of 2tr and ch2 for ch1. **Round 2:** work as Round 1. **Round 3:** work 1PS instead of 3tr and ch2 for ch1. **Round 4:** work as Round 1.

variations
twinkle

see base design on page 215

variation 2
Mix it up Using yarn B, work as given for main pattern, using 2 ends of yarn together; add a lurex yarn for a touch of sparkle or work each point in a different colour.

variation 4
Starfish Using yarn C, work Round 1 as given for main pattern. **Round 2:** * ch10, 1dc into 3rd ch from hook, work as follows into the rem 9ch, 1dc into next ch, 1htr into next 2ch, 1tr into next 2ch, 1dtr into last 2ch, sk1, ss into next st, repeat from * to end, join with ss into base of ch10. Fasten off.

variation 3
Sun Using yarn C work Round 1 as given for main pattern. **Round 2:** ch3 (counts as 1tr), 1tr into base of ch, * 2tr into next st, rep from * to end, join with ss into top of ch3. Complete the motif by working as given for Round 2 of main pattern.

variation 5
Points Using yarn C, work as given for Variation 3, on the next round make 1st point as main pattern, then 2nd point as variation 4, alternate between the 2 patterns until all points have been worked. Fasten off.

variations

solar

see base design on page 216

variation 2

Half treble crochet Work as given for main pattern, working in htr throughout and working ch2 for turning.

variation 3

Treble crochet Work as given for main pattern, working in tr throughout and working ch3 for turning.

variation 4

Spike stitch Work as given for main pattern for Rows 1–4. Join in yarn B and work next round as follows. **Round 5:** ch1, 1dc into 1st 2sts, * work 1 spike into next st inserting hook 2 rows down, 1dc into next 2sts, work 1 spike inserting hook 3 rows down, 1dc into next 2sts, rep from * to end, join with ss into tch. Fasten off yarn B and join yarn A back in, work 6 points as given for main pattern.

variation 5

Shooting star Work as in main block, working Rounds 1–4 in yarns F, A, D and B, work a dc around the 5 points of the star using E. At the end, add 12 cm (5 inch) lengths of yarn to 1 side to create the tail.

variations

galaxy

see base design on page 219

variation 2

Cluster centre star Using yarn C, ch6, join with ss. **Round 1:** ch3, 2tr cl into ring. * ch2, 3tr cl into ring. Repeat from * 6 more times. Ch2, ss into ch3 to join. Ss along to ch sp. **Round 2:** ch3 (counts as first tr), 2tr. ** ch1, 3tr into next ch sp. Repeat from ** around. Ch1, join with ss. **Round 3:** ch3 (counts as first tr), 2tr, ch4, 3tr into ch sp. Into each ch sp work 3tr, ch4, 3tr. Join with ss.

variation 3

Five-pointed star Using yarn E, ch4, join with ss. **Round 1:** ch3 (counts as first tr), 9tr into ring. Join with ss. **Round 2:** ch3 (counts as first tr), 1tr in first st. 2tr into each st around. Join with ss to top of ch3. **Round 3:** ch3 (counts as first tr), 1tr into first st. * ch2, sk1, 2tr into next. Repeat from * around. Ch2, ss to ch3 to join. **Round 4:** ch3, 2tr, ch3, 3tr into first ch sp, 1dc into next. * 3tr, ch3, 3tr into next ch sp, 1dc into next. Repeat from * around. Join with ss to ch3. Fasten off. Weave in ends.

variation 4

Solid granny star Using yarn B, ch5, join with ss. **Round 1:** ch3 (counts as first tr), work 2tr cl into ring. * ch3, 3tr cl into ring. Repeat from * 3 more times. Join with ss into top of ch2. **Round 2:** ss along to next ch sp. Ch3 (counts as first tr) 2tr, ch2, 3tr in ch sp. * 3tr, ch2, 3tr in next ch sp. Repeat from * 3 more times, join with ss in top of ch3. **Round 3:** ss into next st, ch3, 1tr in next st. * 3tr, ch2, 3tr into next ch sp, 1tr in each of next 2sts, sk2, 1tr in each of next 2sts. Repeat from * 3 more times, join with ss in top of ch3. **Round 4:** ss into next st, ch3, 1tr in each of next 3sts. 3tr, ch2, 3tr in next corner ch sp. 1tr in each of next 4sts, skip next 2sts, * 1tr in each of next 4sts, 3tr, ch2, 3tr in next corner ch sp, 1tr in each of next 4sts, skip next 2sts*. Repeat from * to * 3 more times. Join with ss in top of ch3. Fasten off.

variation 5

Cluster star Using yarn D, work Round 1 as per Variation 2. **Round 2:** ch3, 3tr cl into ch sp. * ch3, 4tr cl into ch sp. Repeat from * around. Ch3, join with ss. Ss along to next ch sp. **Round 3:** ch3 (counts as first tr) work 3tr cl, ch5, 4tr cl into next ch sp. Work * 4tr cl, ch5, 4tr cl into each ch sp. Repeat from * around. Join with ss. Fasten off.

flora

see base design on page 220

variation 2

Open flower Using yarn C, ch 3, join with ss to form ring. **Round 1:** ch5 (counts as 1tr and 2ch), * 1tr, ch2, rep from * to end, join with ss to 3rd of ch5. **Round 2:** work as Round 2 of main pattern. Fasten off.

variation 4

Lazy daisy Using yarn B, ch 4, join with ss to form ring. **Round1:** * ch4, 1dtr into ring, ch4, ss to ring, rep from * 4 more times. Fasten off.

variation 3

Puff stitch violet Using yarn D, ch4, join with ss to form ring. **Round 1:** ch1 (counts as 1 tr), 12dc into ring, join with ss into ch1. Fasten off yarn D and join in yarn E. **Round 2:** ch1, 1 puff st into next st, ss into next st, rep from * to end. Fasten off.

variation 5

Pretty violet Using yarn D, ch 4, join with ss to form ring. **Round 1:** work as round 1 of main pattern. **Round 2:** * ch4, sk1, 1dc into next st, rep from * ending last rep with ss into base of ch4. **Round 3:** ch1 (counts as 1ch), 4tr into 1st ch 4 loop, * ss into next st, 5tr into next ch4 loop, rep from * to end, ss into ch1.

variations

in bloom

see base design on page 223

variation 2

Lacy flower coaster Using yarn D, ch3, join with ss to form a ring. **Rounds 1–2:** work as given for main pattern. **Round 3:** ch4 (counts as 1tr and ch1), 1tr into next st, ch1, * 1tr into next st, ch1, rep from * to end, join with ss into ch1. **Round 4:** ch3 (counts as 1tr), * 2tr into next ch sp, 1tr into next st, rep from * to last ch sp, 2tr into ch sp, join with ss into ch3. **Round 5:** * sk3, 7tr into next st, sk3, ss into next st, rep from * to ending last rep with ss into 1st of 7tr at beg of round.

variation 3

Daisy Using yarn B, ch3, join with ss to form a ring. **Rounds 1–3:** work as given for Variation 1. **Round 4:** ch3 (counts as 1st tr), 1tr into each to end, join with ss into ch3. Fasten off yarn B and join in yarn H. **Round 5:** * ch8, ss int 2nd ch from hook, ss into each of the rem 5ch, ss into next 2sts, rep from * to end, join with ss into base of ch8 (20 stems). **Round 6:** * work the following up stem (1dc into next 2 sts, 1htr into next 2sts, 1tr into next st), 7tr into top st, work the following back down stem (1tr into next 2sts, 1htr into next 2sts, 1dc into next 2sts), rep from * working around each stem to end, join with ss into base of 1st dc. Fasten off.

variation 4

Sunflower Using yarn H, ch3, join with ss to form a ring. **Rounds 1–3:** work as given for Variation 1. Fasten off yarn H and join in yarn I. **Round 4:** ch3 (counts as 1tr), 1 tr into same st, sk1, ch1 * 2tr into next st, sk1, ch1 rep from * to end, join with ss into ch3. **Round 5:** 3tr, 3ch, 3tr into 1st ch sp, * ss into next ch sp work (3tr, ch3, 3tr) into next ch sp, rep from * ending last rep with ss into top of 1st of st at beg of round.

variation 5

Granny flower Using yarn C, ch5, join with ss to form a ring. **Round 1:** ch2 (counts as 1tr), 2trtog (1st cluster worked), * ch2, 1tr cl into ring, rep from * 6 more times, 2ch, ss into top of 1st cluster. **Round 2:** ss into 1st ch sp, ch3, 2tr into same sp, ch1 * 3 tr into next ch sp, ch1, rep from * to end. **Round 3:** ss into next 3 sts and ch sp, ch3 (counts as 1tr), 2 tr, ch1, 3tr into same sp, ch1, * (3tr, ch3, 3tr) into next ch sp, ch1, rep from * to end, join with ss into ch3. **Round 4:** ss into next st, 5tr into next ch sp, * sk1, ss into next st, sk1, 5tr into next ch sp, rep from * ending last rep with ss into 1st of 5 tr at beg of round. Fasten off.

variations

posy

see base design on page 224

variation 2
Starry flower Using yarn C, ch4, join with ss. **Round 1:** ch2 (counts as 1htr), 11htr into ring, join with ss into ch2. **Round 2:** * ch1, work (1htr, 1tr, 1htr) into next ch1, ss into next st, rep from * to end, ss into ch1. Work next round at the back of work to create 6 loops. **Round 3:** ch3, sk petal, 1dc into back of ss, rep from * to end, join with ss into ch3. **Round 4:** * Ch1, work (1htr, 1tr, 1dtr, 1tr, 1htr) into ch3 loop, ch1, 1dc into next st, rep from * to end, join with ss into ch1.

variation 3
Pansy Using yarn B, ch4, join with ss to form a ring. **Round 1:** *ch4, 3dtr into ring, ch4, ss to ring (1st petal worked), rep from * 3 more times making 4 petals in total. Work next round at the back of work to create 4 loops. **Round 2:** ch1, ss into back of next st, ch1, 1dc into next st, * ch2, work 1dc into back of the middle st of next petal, rep from * ending last rep with ss into ch1. **Round 3:** * work (ch4, 4dtr, ch4) into ch2loop, ss into next st, rep from * ending last rep with ss into base of ch4. Fasten off.

variation 4
Offset petal flower Using yarn D, Ch4, join with ss to form a ring. **Round 1:** Ch5 (counts as 1tr and ch2), 1tr into ring, * ch2, 1tr into ring, rep from * 3 more times, ch2, join with ss into 3rd of ch5. **Round 2:** Ch1, * work (1dc, 3tr, 1dc) into ch2 loop, rep from * to end, join with ss into ch1. Work next round at the back of work to create 6 loops. **Round 3:** Ss into back of next 2sts, ch1, 1dc into back of next st, * ch3, sk4, 1dc into back of next st, rep from * to ending last rep with ss into ch1. **Round 4:** ch1, * work (1dc, 5tr, 1dc) into ch2 loop, rep from * to end, join with ss into ch1. Fasten off.

variations

fall in love

see base design on page 227

variation 2

Clover leaf Using yarn B, ch5, join with ss to form ring. **Round 1:** * ch3, 2tr into ring, ch3, ss into ring, rep from * twice more, ch3 to make stalk. Fasten off.

variation 3

Maple leaf Using yarn D, ch4, join with ss to form ring. **Round 1:** ch3 (counts as 1tr), 11tr into ring, join with ss into ch3. **Round 2:** ch3, 1tr into first st, 2tr into each of the next 2sts, ch7, MP – ss into 3rd ch from hook, work into rem ch4 as follows (1dc, 1htr, 2tr, 3dtr around stem of tr), ss into next st, * ch8, MP – ss into 3rd ch from hook, work into rem ch4 as follows (1dc, 1htr, 2tr, 3dtr into last ch), sk1, ss into next st, rep from * 3 more times, work 2tr into each st to end, join with ss into ch3, ch4 for stalk. Fasten off.

variation 4

Oak leaf Using yarn C, ch12. **Round 1:** 5tr into 3rd ch from hook, ss into next ch, sk2, ss into next st, 4tr into next ch, ss into next ch, work (ch4, ss into next ch) twice, MP into next st, ch4, ss into same pl, ch4, ss into next st, sk1, 4tr into next st, sk1, ss into next st, sk1, 5tr into next st, join with ss into last ch, ch4 to form stalk.

variation 5

Tiny leaf Using yarn B, ch4, join with ss to form ring. **Round 1:** ch1, work (2dc, 2htr, 1tr, 1dtr) into ring, MP, then work (1dtr, 1tr, 2htr, 2ch) into ring, ss into ch1.

rectangles

see base design on page 228

variation 2

Ribbed rectangles Using yarn D, ch30+3 for turning. **Row 1:** 1tr into 4th ch from hook, 1tr into each ch to end, turn. **Row 2:** ch3, 1tr into back loop of 1st st, 1tr into back loop of each st to end, turn. Repeat Row 2 twice more. Fasten off.

variation 3

Rectangle in the round Using yarn D, ch20+3 for turning. **Round 1:** ch3, 1tr into 4th ch from hook, 1tr into each ch to end, work (ch3, 2tr, ch3) into same ch, ch3, work 1tr into underside of each ch to end, work (1tr, ch3, 2tr) into same ch, ch3, join with ss into ch3. **Round 2:** ch4 (counts as 1tr and ch1), * sk1, 1tr into next st, ch1, rep from * to ch3sp, work (2tr, ch3, 1tr) into ch3sp, ch1, 1tr in between 2tr, ch1, work (1tr, ch3, 2tr)into next ch3sp, ** sk1, 1tr into next st, ch1, rep from ** to ch3sp work (2tr, ch3, 1tr) into next ch3sp, ch1, 1tr in between 2tr, ch1, work (1tr, 3ch, 2tr into last ch3sp, ch1, ss into 3rd of ch4. Fasten off.

variation 4

Granny rectangles Using yarn A, ch 20+3 for turning. **Round 1:** ch3, 1tr into first ch, * sk2, 3tr into next, rep from * 5 times, sk2, work (2tr, ch3, 3tr, 3ch, 2tr) into last ch (corner worked), work back along the underside of ch to match top as foll: ** sk2, 3tr into next ch, rep from ** 5 times, work (2tr, ch3, 3tr) into 1st ch, ss into ch3. Fasten off yarn A and join in yarn E ch3sp. **Round 2:** ch3, 2tr, ch3, 3tr into corner space, work 3tr into each ch sp and 3tr, ch3, 3tr into ch ch3sp around the outer edge. Fasten off.

variation 5

Puff stitch rectangles Using yarn E, ch30+1 for turning. **Row1:** 1dc into 2nd ch from hook, 1tr into each ch to end, turn. **Row 2:** ch2, sk1, work 1 puff st into next st, * ch1, sk1, work puff st into next, rep from * to end. **Rows 3–4:** work as Row 2. **Row 5:** ch3, sk1, 1dc into each st to end. Fasten off.

variations

diamonds are forever

see base design on page 231

variation 2

Treble crochet Using yarn B, ch4. **Row 1:** 2tr into 4th ch from hook, turn. **Rows 2–10:** increase as given for main pattern, working tr throughout and ch3 for turning. **Rows 11–20 (dec):** ch3 (counts as 1tr), sk1, tr2tog, 1tr into each st until last 3sts, tr2tog, 1tr into last st, turn.

variation 3

Spike stitch diamond Using yarn D, work as given for main pattern keeping inc and dec correct. Work every 4th row as spike stitch in yarn A. **Spike rows:** work 2sts as main pattern, * 1sp st (work dc into same st 1 row below), dc into next st, rep to last 2sts, 1dc into last 2, turn.

variation 4

Double treble crochet diamond Using yarn C, ch5. **Row 1:** 2dtr into 4th ch from hook, turn. **Rows 2–6 (inc):** work as given for main pattern, working dtr throughout and ch4 for turning. **Rows 7–12 (dec):** ch4 (counts as 1dtr), sk2, 1dtr into each st to last 2sts, sk1, 1dtr in last, do not work into tch, turn.

variation 5

Diamond in a box Work diamond as per main pattern, inc to Row 10 before dec. Fasten off. Join in new yarn on sideways 'point', 1dc to lock in the new yarn. **Round 1:** with diamond on its side, ch4, work 1dtr into the st that sits directly below the hook, ch4, work 1dtr into the side of the bottom point of the diamond. Turn. Ch3 (counts as 1tr), 2tr into the ch4 sp, 3tr into top of dtr, 3tr into next ch sp, ch3, 1dc into dc. Ch4, work 1dtr into st directly below hook, ch4, 1trtr into side of opposite point of diamond. Turn. Ch3 (counts as 1tr), 2tr into ch sp, 3tr into dtr, 3tr into ch sp. Join in yarn on opposite side of diamond, repeat Row 1 on that side. Turn, then work as granny square, working 3tr into ch sp, and 3tr, ch3, 3tr for corners. Fasten off yarn B.

octagons

see base design on page 232

variation 2

Spider's web Using yarn B, ch5, join with ss to form ring. **Round 1:** work as main pattern. **Round 2:** ch3 (counts as 1tr), 2tr into same sp, ch2, sk1, 3tr into next st ch2, rep from * to end; join with ss in to ch3. **Round 3:** ch3 (counts as 1tr), 1tr in next 2sts, * (1tr, ch 2, 1tr) in next ch2, 1tr in next 3sts, rep from * 6 more times, 1tr in next ch2sp, ch2, join with a ss in to ch3. **Round 4:** ch3 (counts as 1tr), 1tr in next 3sts, * (1tr, ch2, 1tr) into next ch2 sp, 1tr into next 5sts, rep from * 6 more times, (1tr, ch2, 1tr) into last ch2sp, join with ss in to ch . Fasten off.

variation 3

Striped octagon Work as given for main pattern, working Round 1 in yarn A, Round 2 in yarn B, Round 3 in yarn C and Round 4 in yarn D. Fasten off.

variation 4

Granny octagon Using yarn A, ch5, join with ss to form a ring. **Round 1:** ch3 (counts as 1tr), 2tr into ring, ch2, * 3tr, into ring, ch2, rep from * twice more, join with ss into ch3, ss into next 2sts and 1st ch2sp. Fasten off yarn A and join in yarn E. **Round 2:** ch3 (counts as 1tr), 2tr, 2ch, 3tr into same sp, ch1 * work (3tr, ch2, 3tr) into next ch2sp, ch1, rep from * to end, join with ss into ch3, ss into next 2sts and 1st ch2sp, join with ss into ch3. Fasten off yarn E and join in yarn C. **Round 3:** ch3 (counts as 1tr), 3tr into same sp, ch2, * 4tr into next ch sp, rep from * to end, join with ss into ch3, ss into next 2sts and 1st ch2sp, join with ss into ch3. Fasten off yarn C and join in yarn D. **Round 4:** ch3 (counts as 1tr),1tr into 1st ch2 sp, ch2, 2tr into same sp, * ch1, 2tr in middle of next 4sts, ch1, work (2tr, ch2, 2tr) into next ch2sp, rep from * 6 more times, ch1, 2tr in middle of last 4sts, ch1, join with ss into ch3. Fasten off yarn.

variations

henry

variation 2

Granny hexagon Using yarn B, ch4, join with a ss to form a ring. **Round 1:** ch3 (counts as 1tr), 2tr into the ring, * ch2, 3tr, rep from * 4 more times, ch2, join with a ss in to ch3, turn. Fasten off yarn B and join in yarn A. **Round 2:** ch3 (counts as 1tr), 2tr, ch2, 3tr into 1st ch2sp, * ch1, 3tr, 2ch, 3tr into the next ch2sp, rep from * 4 more times, ch1, join with a ss into 3ch, turn. Fasten off yarn A and join in yarn C. **Round 3:** ch3 (counts as 1tr), 2tr, into 1st ch sp, * ch1, 3tr, 2ch, 3tr into the next ch sp, ch1 **, 3 tr into next ch sp, rep from * 4 more times, ending last rep at **, join with ss into ch3.

variation 3

Starburst Using yarn C, ch6, join with ss to form a ring. **Round 1:** ch3 (counts as 1tr), 11tr into ring, join with a ss into ch3. Fasten off yarn C and join in yarn A. **Round 2:** ch3, 1tr into same st, * 3tr into next st, 2tr into next st, rep from * 4 more times, 3tr into last st, join with ss into ch3. Fasten off yarn A and join in yarn B. **Ss** ch3, 1tr into same st, 1tr into next 2sts, * work (2tr, 2ch, 2tr) into next st, 1tr into next 4 sts, rep from * 4 more times, 2tr, 2ch, 2tr into next st, 1tr into next st, join with ss into ch3. Fasten off.

variations

see base design on page 235

variation 4

Spiral Hexagon Using yarn D, ch6, join with a ss into a ring. **Round 1:** ch3, 17tr in ring, join sl st to top of ch2. **Round 2:** ch3, tr in same st, * ch2, sk2, 3tr innext st, rep from * 4 more times, ch2, tr in same space as 1st tr, sl st to top of ch3. **Round 3:** ch3, 1tr in same st, * ch3, 2tr in ch sp, 1tr in 1st tr of group, 2tr in next tr, skip next tr, rep from * 4 more times, ch3, 2tr last ch sp, tr in tr, join with sl st to top of ch2. **Round 4:** ch3, tr in same st, * ch4, 2tr in ch sp, 1tr in next 3sts, 2tr in next tr, skip next tr, rep from * 4 more times, ch4, 2tr in last ch sp, 1tr in last 3sts, join with sl st to top of ch2. **Round 5:** ch3, tr in same st,* ch5, 2tr in ch sp, 1tr into next 5sts, 2tr in next tr, skip next tr, rep from * 4 more times, ch5, 2tr inlast ch sp, 1tr in last 5sts, join with sl st to top of ch2. Fasten off.

variation 5

African flower hexagon Using yarn C, ch5 and join with a ss into a ring. **Round 1:** ch3, 1tr into the ring, * ch1, 2tr in to the ring, rep from * 4 more times, ch1 join with a ss into the 3rd of the 3 ch. **Round 2:** join in D, ch3, 1tr, ch1, 2tr into same st, * 2tr, 1ch, 2tr, into next ch sp, rep from * 4 more times, join with a ss into 3rd of 3ch. **Round 3:** ch3, 6tr into same st, * 7tr into the next ch sp, repeat from * 4 more times, join with ss into 3rd of 3ch. **Round 4:** join in B, ch1, work a dc into each of the 7tr of the previous round, work a tr into the the ch sp of the previous round, in between each of the petals. **Round 5:** join in yarn A, ch3, tr into each of next 3st, * work 1tr, 1ch, 1tr into next sp, work a tr into each of the next 6 st, rep from * 4 more times, 1tr into the next 3st, join with a ss into the 3rd of the 3ch. Fasten off.

variations

meadow hexagons

see base design on page 236

variation 2

Daisy centre hexagon Using yarn C, ch6, join with ss to form ring. **Round 1:** work as given for main pattern. Break off yarn C and join in yarn A. **Round 2:** ch5, 2trtr into 1st st, ch5, ss into next st, * ch5, 2trtr into next st, ch5, ss into next st, rep from * ending last rep with ss into back loop of base of ch5 at beg of round. Break off yarn A and join in yarn E. Work Rounds 3–7 as given for main pattern. Fasten off.

variation 3

Dahlia centre hexagon Using yarn G, ch 4, join with ss to form ring. **Round 1:** work as given for main pattern. **Round 2:** ch3, 1 popcorn st into 1st sc, * ch3, ss into next st, ch3, 1 popcorn st into next st, rep from * ending last st with ss into base of ch 3. Break off yarn G and join in yarn E. Work Rounds 3–7 as given for main pattern. Fasten off.

variation 4

Violet centre hexagon Using yarn F, ch4, join with ss to form ring. **Round 1:** ch1 (counts as 1dc), 5dc into ring, join with ss into ch1. **Round 2:** * ch1, 1 puff st into 1st st, 1 puff st into next st, rep from * to end, join with ss into top of 1st puff st. Break off yarn F and join in yarn E. Work Rounds 3–7 as given for main pattern. Fasten off.

variation 5

Marigold centre hexagon Using yarn C, ch 4, join with ss to form ring. **Round 1:** as given for main pattern. **Round 2:** * ch8, ss into 3rd ch from hook, work back down rem ch's as follows (1dc into next ch, 1htr into next 4ch, sk1, ss into next st, rep from * ending last rep with ss into base of ch8. Break off yarn C and join in yarn E. Work Rounds 3–7 as given for main pattern. Fasten off.

cheep cheep

see base design on page 239

variation 2

Three-coloured stripes Work as given for main pattern; Rows 1–2 in yarn A, Rows 3–4 in yarn B, Rows 5–6 in yarn C form stripe sequence, keeping pattern correct rep until 14 rows have been worked.

variation 4

Bobbles Work as given for main pattern using yarn C, but with changes to the following rows. **Row 3:** work 3rd st in yarn B. **Row 5:** work 4th st in B, 6th st in A and 8th st in B. **Row 7:** work 4th st in yarn B. **Row 9:** as Row 5. **Row 11:** work 3rd st in yarn B. **Row 13:** work 5th st in yarn B.

variation 3

Chick Work as given for main pattern; attach yarn C to the edge at Row 9 then work 3dc, turn work 2 dc, turn, work 1dc. Fasten off. Add a little stitch for the eye.

variation 5

With an edge Work as given for main pattern, then join in yarn A. Work edge as follows: ch1, 2dc in 1st st, * 1dc in next st, 1dc in to next st, rep from * to end, ss into ch1.

variations

beachcombing

see base design on page 240

variation 2
Shell Using yarn C, ch4, join with ss to form ring. **Row 1:** 8dc into ring, do not join with ss, work (2htr in back loop of next st) 5 times, (2tr into back loop of next st) 9 times, (2dtr in to back loop of next st) 7 times, (1dtr into back of next st, 2dtr into back loop of next st) 7 times, 1dtr into back loop of next st, 2dtr into back of next st, 2dtr into back of next st. Fasten off.

variation 3
Tri-colour Using yarn D, ch6 join with ss to form a ring. **Row 1:** ch1, work * (1dc, 1htr, 4tr) in a ring, drop D, leave large loop, rep from * using yarn E and F. **Row 2:** pick up D, * work 2tr into each of the next 6sts, drop D, rep from * rep from * using yarns E and F. **Row 3:** Pick up yarn A, * work (1tr into next 3sts, 2tr into next st) 3 times, drop D, rep from * using E and F. **Row 4:** pick up A, * work (1tr into next 4sts, 2tr into next st) 3 times, drop D, rep from * using E and F. **Row 5:** pick up A, * work (1tr into next 5sts, 2tr, ch1, 2tr into next st) 3 times, drop D, rep from * using E and F. **Row 6:** pick up A, * work 1htr, 1dc, ss into next st, fasten off, rep from * using E and F.

variation 4
Spiral granny square Using yarn D, ch4 join with ss to form ring. **Round 1:** * ch1, 1dc, 1htr, 2tr into ring, drop D, rep from * using yarns E, F and G. **Round 2:** pick up D, * work 2tr in next st, 1tr, 1htr, 2tr in next st, 1tr, rep from * using E, F and G. **Round 3:** Pick up A, * ch2, 1tr in next st, 1tr, 2tr in each next 2sts, 1tr into next 2sts, rep from * using E, F and G. **Round 4:** pick up A, * work (3tr, ch2, 3tr) in ch2sp, 1tr in each of the next 6sts three times, rep from * using E, F G. **Round 5:** pick up A, * work (3tr, ch1, 3tr) in 2chsp, 1tr in each of the next 5sts, rep from * using E, F and G.

variation 5
Hoopla: work as given for Variation 3 but with hoopla yarn and 10mm hook.

274 variations

variations

flutterby

see base design on page 243

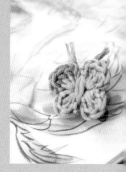

variation 2

In the air Using yarn D, ch4, join with ss to form a ring. Round 1: * ch3, 3tr into ring, ch4, ss into ring, rep from * 3 times more. Fasten off and finish as per main pattern.

variation 4

On the breeze Using yarn E, ch4, join with ss to form a ring. Round 1: ch4, 3dtr into ring, ch3, ss into ring, ch3, 3dtr into ring, ch4, ss into ring,* ch3, 3tr into ring, ch3, ss into ring, rep from * once more to end. Fasten off and finish as per main pattern.

variation 3

Featherweight Using yarn F, ch4, join with ss to form a ring. **Round 1:** * ch4, 3dc into ring, ch4, ss into ring, rep from * once more, ** ch3, 2sc into ring, ch3, ss into ring, rep from ** once more to end. Fasten off and finish as per main pattern.

variation 5

Migration Using yarn G, ch4, join with ss to form a ring. Round 1: * ch4, 3dtr into ring, ch4, ss into ring, rep from * once more. * ch4, 2dtr into loop, ch4, ss into ring, rep from * once more to end. Fasten off and finish as per main pattern.

variations

bunting

see base design on page 244

variation 2
Bobble stripe Using yarn B, work triangle as main pattern using dc throughout and ch1 for turning. Work dec on every 2nd row with dc2tog at beg and end of row. Work bobbles in yarn A on every 3rd row as follows. **Row 4:** ch1, 1dc into 1st st, * MB in next st, 1dc into next 4sts, rep from * once more 1dc into last st, turn. **Row 7:** ch1, 1dc into 1st 2sts, MB, 4dc, MB, 1dc into each st to end, turn. **Row 10:** work as Row 7. **Row 13:** ch1, 1dc into 1st st, MB, 3dc, MB, 1dc, turn. **Row 16:** ch1, 1dc into 1st 2sts, MB, 1dc into each st to end, turn.

variation 4
Granny stripe Using yarn C, ch4. **Row 1:** 3tr into 3th ch from hook, turn. **Row 2:** ch3 (counts as 1tr), 1tr into 1st st, ch1, sk1, 2tr into last st, turn. **Row 3:** ch4 (counts as 1tr and ch1), 3tr into ch1sp, ch1, 1tr into top of tch, turn. **Row 4:** ch3 (counts as 1tr), 2tr into ch1sp, ch1, 3tr into next ch1sp, turn. Continue working in pattern as set, working 2tr into 1st of 3tr group at the beg of row, and 2tr into last st of 3tr group at end of row, and working 3tr's into ch1sp.

variation 3
Spike stitch stripes Work Row 1 as per main pattern but in dc, as per Variation 2, in yarn B. Work 4 rows. **Spike stitch row:** change to yarn C. Work 1 dc, 1 spike stitch (SP) across on right side only. Work 3 more rows of dc in yarn C, then change back to yarn B. Dec on alternate rows. Repeat SP row, changing colour every 4 rows.

variation 5
Stripes Work triangle as main pattern using dc throughout and ch1 for turning. Work dec on every 2nd row with dc2tog at beg and end of row. Keeping pattern correct work a 2-row stripe throughout starting with yarn C, then yarn D.

variations

stella

see base design on page 247

variation 2

Solid Tr triangle Using yarn C, ch4, join with ss to form a ring. **Round 1:** work as given for main pattern. **Round 2:** ch3 (counts as 1tr), 1tr into each of the next 2sts, * 2tr, ch3, 2tr into 1st ch3sp, 1tr into next 3sts, rep from * once more, 2tr, ch3, 2tr into last ch3sp, ch1, join with ss into ch3. **Round 3:** ch3 (counts as 1tr), 1tr into each of the next 4sts, * 2tr, ch3, 2tr into 1st ch3sp, 1tr into next 7sts, rep from * once more, 2tr, ch3, 2tr into last ch3sp, ch1, join with ss into ch3.

variation 4

Shawl triangle Using yarn A Ch 4, join with ss. **Row 1:** ch4 (counts as 1tr and ch1), 3tr into ring, ch2, 3tr into ring, ch1, 1tr into ring, turn. **Row 2:** ch4 (counts as 1tr and ch1), 3tr into ch sp, ch1, work (3tr, 2ch, 3tr) into corner ch3sp, ch1, 3tr into ch sp, ch1, 1tr into ch sp, turn. **Row 3:** ch4 (counts as 1tr and ch1), work (3tr into next ch sp) twice, ch1, work (3tr, 2ch, 3tr) into corner ch3sp, ch1, work(3tr into ch sp) twice, ch1, 1tr into ch sp, turn.

variation 3

Lacy triangle Using yarn B, ch4, join with ss to form a ring. **Round 1:** work as given for main pattern. **Round 2:** ch3 (counts as 1st tr) 2tr into 1st st, 1tr into next st, * ch2 (2tr, 4ch, 2tr) into next ch3 sp (1st corner worked), 2ch, ** 1tr into next st, 2tr into next st, 1tr into next st, rep from * twice more ending last rep at ** join with ss into top of ch3. **Round 3:** ch5, sk1, * 1tr into next st, *ch1, sk1, 1tr into next ch 2sp, ch2, work (2tr, ch4, 2tr) into next ch3sp, ch2, 1tr into next ch2sp **, ch1, sk1, rep from * ending last rep at **, ch1, ss into ch3.

variation 5

Solid shawl triangle Using yarn C work as given for Variation 4, working 1tr into top of every st rather than working 3tr into ch sp and working 2tr, ch2, 2tr into corners, and 2tr into ch sp.

variations

big love

see base design on page 248

variation 2
Back and forth method
Row 1: Using yarn E, ch2. **Row 1:** 2dc into 2nd ch from hook, turn. **Row 2:** ch1, 1dc into 1st st, 2dc into 2nd st, turn.
Row 3 (inc): ch1, 1dc into 1st st, 1dc into each st to last st, 2dc, turn. Repeat last row until 19sts. Shape top as follows. **Next row:** 1dc into 9sts, turn. Next row (dec): vh1, sk1, 1dc into each st to last 2sts, sk1, 1dc into last, turn. Repeat last row until 2sts. Fasten off. Rejoin yarn to rem sts and repeat shape top, do not break off yarn. Work 1dc into each st and row around the outer edge of heart working 3dc into point.

variation 3
Picot edge heart
Smaller heart: using yarn A, work as main pattern till 13sts. Work, decrease sections over 6sts, but do not make dc border. Fasten off yarn A, and join in yarn B at base of heart. **Picot edge:** * ch3, ss into 3rd ch from hook, sk1, ss into next st, rep from * to end. Fasten off.

variation 4
Granny edge heart
Work smaller or large back-and-forth heart pattern. Join in yarn D at base of heart.
Granny edge: ch3, 2tr into 1st st, * sk2, 3tr into next st, working the 3tr into the end of every 2nd row of heart, rep from * to end, join with ss into ch3.

variation 5
Lacy edge heart Work smaller or large back-and-forth heart pattern. Join in yarn B at base of heart. **Lace edge:** 1dc into 1st st, * ch3, sk2, 1dc into next st, rep from * to end. Fasten off.

kind hearts

see base design on page 251

variation 2

Granny centre heart Using yarn A, ch3, join with ss to form a ring. **Round 1:** ch3, 2tr into ring. * 3ch, 3tr into ring, rep from * twice more, ch3 join with ss into top of 3ch. **Round 2:** sk1, 7dtr into next st, ch2, ss into 1st ch3sp, ch2, sk1, 7dtr into next st, ss into next ch3sp, ss into next (3sts, 3ch, 3sts), ss into top of 1st of 7dtr. Fasten off.

variation 4

Loop centre heart Using yarn B, ch4, join with ss to form a ring. **Round 1:** ch1 (counts as 1tr), 11dc into ring, join with ss into ch1. **Round 2:** ch1, 2dc into 1st st, *1 dc into next 2 sts, 3dc into next. Repeat from * twice more 1dc into last 2sts. Join with ss. **Round 3:** ss into 1st corner, sk2, 7tr into nest st, ss into next corner, sk2, 7tr into next st, ss into each of the last 2 corners. Fasten off.

variation 3

Solid centre heart Use yarn C. **Row 1:** ch7, 1htr into 3rd ch from hook, 1htr into next 4sts, turn. **Row 2:** Ch2, 1htr into each st to end. Repeat row 2 once more. **Row 4:** Sk1, 7dtr into next st, ch2, ss into next st, ch2, 7dtr into next st, ss into top of dtr.

variation 5

Teeny tiny heart Using yarn D, ch5, join with ss. **Round 1:** ch2, work (4tr, 1dtr, 4tr) into ring, ch2, ss into ring. Fasten off.

pot holder

variation 2

Diamond Work as pattern below in stripe sequence in the following yarns. **Round 1–2:** N. **Round 3:** O. **Round 4:** P. **Round 5:** O. **Rounds 6–8:** N. ch5, join with ss to form ring. **Round 1:** ch3 (counts as 1tr), 2tr into ring, ch2, * 3tr into ring, ch3, rep from * twice more, join with ss into ch3. **Round 2:** ch3, 1tr into 1st 2sts, work (2tr, ch3, 2tr) into 1st ch3sp (1st corner worked), * 1tr into next 3sts, work (2tr, ch3, 2tr) into next ch3sp, rep from * twice more, join with ss into ch3. **Round 3:** ch3, 1tr into each st to 1st ch3sp, work (2tr, ch3, 2tr) into ch3sp, * 1tr into each st to next ch3sp, work (2tr, ch3, 2tr) into next ch3sp, rep from * twice more, work 1tr into each st to end, join with ss into ch3. Repeat last row 3 more times. **Round 7:** ch1, 1dc into each st to 1st ch3sp, work 4dc into ch3sp, * 1dc into each st to next ch3sp, work 4dc into next ch3sp, rep from * twice more, work 1dc into each st to end, join with ss into ch3. **Round 8:** ch1, 1dc into next 14 sts, ch2, 1dc into next 27sts, ch16, *1dc into next 27sts, ch2, rep from * once more, 1dc into each st to end, join with ss into ch3.

variation 3

Square Using yarn Q, ch4, join with ss to form ring. **Round 1:** ch3 (counts as 1tr), 11tr into ring, join with a ss into 3ch. **Round 2:** ch3 (counts as 1tr), * work (2tr, 1dtr) into next st, then (1dtr, 2tr) into next st (1st corner worked) **, 1tr into next st, rep from *, 3 more times, ending last ** join with a ss into 3ch. **Round 3:** ch3 (counts as 1tr), 1tr into 1st 2sts, * work (2tr, 1dtr) into next st, then (1dtr, 2tr) into next st (1st corner worked), 1tr into next 5sts, rep from *, 3 more times, ending last rep with 1tr into 3sts, join with a ss into 3ch. Join in yarn R. **Round 4:** ch1, 1dc into 1st 5sts, * work (2dc into next st) twice (1st corner worked), 1dc into next 9sts, rep from * 3 more times, ending last rep with 1dc into last 4sts, join with ss into ch1. Join in yarn Q. **Round 5:** ch3 (counts as 1tr), 1tr into 1st 6sts, * work (2tr, 1dtr) into next st, then (1dtr, 2tr) into next st (1st corner worked), 1tr into next 11sts, rep from *, 3 more times, ending last rep with 1tr into last 5sts, join with ss into 3ch. Join in yarn R. **Round 6:** ch1, 1dc into 1st 8sts, * work (2dc into next st) twice (1st corner worked), 1dc into next 15sts, rep from * 3 more times, ending last rep with 1dc into last 7sts, join with ss into ch1. Join in yarn Q. **Round 7:** ch3 (counts as 1tr), 1tr into 1st 10sts, * work (2tr, 1dtr) into next st, then (1dtr, 2tr) into next st (1st corner worked), 1tr into next 17sts, rep from *, 3 more times, ending last rep with 1tr into last 6sts, join with ss into 3ch. Join in yarn R. **Round 8:** ch1, 1dc into 1st 13sts, * work (2dc into next st) twice (1st corner worked), 1dc into next 21sts, rep from * 3 more times, ending last rep with 1dc into last 9sts, join with ss into ch1. Join in yarn Q. **Round 9:** ch1, 1dc into 1st 15sts, * work (2dc into next st) twice (1st corner worked), 1dc into next 23sts, rep from * 3 more times, ending last rep with 1dc into last 9sts, join with ss into ch1. Fasten off.

variations

see base design on page 252

variation 4

Granny Using yarn C, ch4, join with ss to form ring. **Round 1:** ch3 (counts as 1tr), tr2tog into ring, * ch3, tr3tog, rep from * 6 more times, join with ss into ch3. Ss into 1st ch3sp fasten off yarn C and join in yarn D. **Round 2:** ch3 (counts as 1tr), work (tr2tog, ch3 tr3tog) into same sp (1st corner worked), * work (tr2tog, ch3, tr2tog) into next ch3sp, rep from * 6 more times, join with ss into ch3. Ss into 1st ch3sp fasten off yarn D and join in yarn E. **Round 3:** ch3 (counts as 1tr), work (2tr, ch3, 3tr) into 1st ch3sp, * ch1, 3tr into next ch3sp, ch1 **, work (3tr, ch3, 3tr) into next ch3sp, rep from * 3 more times, ending last rep at **, join with ss into ch3. **Round 4:** ss into next 2sts and ch3sp, ch3 (counts as 1tr), work 2tr, ch3, 3tr into same sp(1st corner worked), * ch1, (3tr into next ch sp, ch1) twice **, work (3tr, ch3, 3tr) into next ch3sp, rep from * 3 more times ending last rep at **, join with ss into ch3. **Round 5:** work as round 4 working (3tr into next ch sp, ch1) 3 times. **Round 6:** work as round 4 working (3tr into next ch sp, ch1) 4 times. **Round 7:** ch1, 1dc into each st to 1st corner, *work (2dc, ch1, 2dc) into corner, work 1dc into each st and ch1sp** up to next corner, rep from * 3more times, ending last rep at **, join with ss into ch1. **Round 8:** ch1, work 1dc into each st and 3dc into corner sp to end, join with ss into ch1.

variation 5

Corner Using yarn F, ch6. **Row 1:** insert hook into 4st from hook, work 3tr, turn. **Row 2:** ch3 (count as 1tr), 1tr into next 3sts, ch1, 1tr into next st, 3tr into tch, turn. **Row 3:** ch3 (counts as 1tr), 1tr into next 3sts, work(1tr, ch3, 1tr) into ch1sp, (corner worked) 1tr into next 3sts st and tch, turn. **Row 4:** ch3, 1tr into each st to corner, work (1tr, ch3, 1tr) into corner, 1tr into each st and tch to end, turn. Row 4 forms pattern; repeat 9 more times in following stripe sequence. **Row 5:** yarn G. **Rows 6–7:** yarn F. **Row 8:** yarn H. **Row 9–10:** yarn F. **Row 11:** yarn J. **Rows 12–13:** yarn F. **Row 14:** work as given for Row 4 working 5tr into corner sp. Fasten off.

variations

blizzard

see base design on page 255

variation 2

Large snowflake Using yarn A, work Rounds 1–3 as given for main pattern. **Round 4:** ss into next st and in ch sp, ch3 (counts as 1tr), 2tr, ch3, 3tr into same sp, * work (3tr, ch3, 3tr), rep from * 6 more times, join with a ss into top of ch3. **Round 5:** ss into next 3sts and ch3sp, * (MP) 5 times, ss into each st along to next ch3sp, rep from * to end, join with ss into ss at beg of round.

variation 3

Hexagonal snowflake Using yarn A, ch6, join with ss to form a ring. **Round 1:** ch4 (counts as 1tr and ch1), * 1tr into ring, ch1 rep from * 10 more times. **Round 2:** ch6 (counts as 1tr and ch3), sk1, 1tr into ch sp, * ch2, 1tr into next ch1sp, ch3, sk1, 1tr into next ch1sp, sk1, rep from * 4 more times, ch2, ss into 3rd of ch3. **Round 3:** ss into 1st ch3 sp, ch3 (counts as 1tr), 4tr into same sp, * ch1,1tr into next ch2sp, ch1, 5tr into next ch3s p, rep from * 4 more times, ch1, 1tr into last ch2sp, ch1, ss into ch3. **Round 4:** ss into in to next 3sts. * MP 3 times, ss into next 2sts, ch1, 1st, ch1 and 3sts, rep from * to end, ss into each st and ch to end, join with ss into ss at beg of round.

variation 4

Picot edge Using yarn A, ch4, join with ss to form a ring. **Round 1:** ch1 (counts as 1tr), 5dc into ring, join with ss into ch1. **Round 2:** ch5, 1tr in to 1st st, * work (1tr, ch2, 1tr) in next st, repeat from * 4 more times, join with ss into 3rd of ch5. **Round 3:** ss into 1st ch2 sp, 3ch (counts as 1tr), 1tr, ch3, 2tr into same ch1sp, work (2tr, ch3, 2tr) next ch2 sp, rep from * 4 more times. **Round 4:** ss into 1st ch3 sp, * (MP) 3 times, ss into next st, MP into next st, ss into next 2sts, rep from * 5 more times, join with ss into ss at beg of round.

variation 5

Flower centre Using yarn A, ch6, join with ss to form a ring. **Round 1:** ch1, * 1dc into ring, ch3, 1 quad-tr into ring, ch3, 1dc into ring (1st petal worked), rep from * 5 more times, ss into ch1. **Round 2:** ss into ch3 and top of 1st petal, * ch2, 1tr in 9th ch from hook, ch3, ss into top of next petal, rep from * to end, join with ss into ss at beg of round. **Round 3:** ss into 1st ch3, * work (5tr, MP, 6tr) into 1st ch8 loop, work (6tr, MP, 6tr) into next ch8 loop, rep from * to end, join with ss into ss at beg of round.

cute crochet

see base design page 256

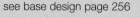

variation 2
Blue moon Work as given for Variation 1, using blue yarn.

variation 4
Cloud Using white yarn, ch18, turn. **Row 1:** 1 dc in 2nd ch from hook, 1 dc into each ch to end, turn. **Rows 2–4:** ch1, sk 1st st, 1 dc into each st to end, turn. **Rows 5–8:** ch1, sk 1st st, 1dc into next 9 sts, turn. Do not turn at the end of Row 8. Turn work clockwise and work the following sts evenly down the long side edge. (1 dc, 2 htr, 2 tr, 2tr, 2 tr, 2 htr), then work back along under side of ch as follows: (3 dc into 1st ch, 1 dc into each ch to end). Work following sts evenly back up short side (3 dc, 2 htr, 2 dtr), work across next 7 sts as follows: (2 dc into next st, sk 2, 5 tr into next st, sk 2, 1dc into next st, ch3, sk 4 rows and ss into 1st st of last 9 sts, work 2 dc into 1st st, sk 3, work 5 tr into next st, ss into dc at beginning.

variation 3
Sun Round 1: ch3, 9 htr into 1st ch, join with ss into 2nd of ch3. **Round 2:** ch2, 1 htr into 1st st, 2 htr into each st to end, join with ss into ch2. **Round 3:** as Round 2. **Round 4:** *ch7, ss into 3rd ch from hook, work back down into remaining 4 ch as follows: 1 htr into 1st ch, 1 tr into next ch, 1 dtr into each of the last ch2, sk 3, ss into next st of circle (1st point worked), ss into next st, rep from * ending last rep with ss into base of ch7. Fasten off.

variation 5
Storm cloud Work as given for Variation 4, using grey yarn for a stormy effect.

index